"We are living in a pivotal moment of courage for survivors of sexual abuse to speak out. We see a massive ground swelling of survivors, unified by their stories, speaking up and saying #metoo. This timely collection is no different; it amplifies the voices of those trans and gender non-conforming people forced into silence because of identity shaming. The courage and bravery shared by these silence breakers becomes an invitation for us to become an ally in the work, to untie our bound hands, to lift our fists in unison, to tear the tape off our mouths, to reclaim our lives and say in unison, #neveragain."

—*sj Miller, author of* Teaching, Affirming, and Recognizing Trans and Gender Creative Youth, *and series co-editor of* Social Justice Across Contexts in Education *and* Queering Teacher Education Across Contexts

"Becoming yourself is the most daring act you will undertake in your lifetime. In some ways it's a bigger deal than being born, because it requires courage, determination, vision and a body that is your own. *Written on the Body* shows us how beautifully it's being done in the 21st century and reminds us that the business of becoming your authentic self is never finished."

—*James Lecesne, co-founder of* The Trevor Project

"As a storytelling organization, we are encouraged by projects like *Written on the Body*. This anthology is in the vanguard of a growing body of storytelling rooted in transgender and non-binary experiences. The acts of writing, reading and sharing these stories have the capacity to build empathy, to heal and to empower more individuals to share their stories as well."

—*Nathan Manske, founder of* I'm From Driftwood

"As trans and non-binary folks, we are often discouraged from advocating for our own bodies, as if we do not know what is best for ourselves. This anthology is filled with such tenderness, resilience and vulnerability; a beautiful love letter to queerness, to otherness, to the power of reclaiming our bodies as our own."

—*Emmett J. Lundberg, writer and filmmaker, creator of* Brothers the series

"It's rare that something can both break your heart and renew your spirit. My heart empathetically broke from the rawness and intimacy these pages hold. As I finished I was left feeling inspired and awestruck at the power of queer people—not just to endure but to use our experiences as a tool to empower others, like these words certainly will."

—*Benjamin O'Keefe, activist and television personality*

"This anthology is an inspirational collection of personal journeys where people share deeply of their pain, healing and triumph. Thank you to all the brave people who contributed their voices. Your courage offers hope and support to those who would otherwise feel alone in their quest to fully own their bodies and define their own identities. You bring us closer to a world where we can transcend the binary and be happy with who we are as individuals."

—*Karmilla Pillay-Siokos, Director of Slutwalk Johannesburg*

"This work is prayer. It is finding family, clarity and yourself in every page. It is a deep breath. Each story takes you closer to understanding what self-love is and how long the paths to ourselves can be. I am so grateful for this book and to each author that blessed its pages."

—*Be Steadwell, queer pop musician and filmmaker*

"*Written on the Body* beautifully paints the picture of what happens to people of trans experience when it comes to sexual assault and violence. This book provides the opportunity to tell our stories in a way that is our own, because these are our experiences. It is a way for us to find some type of healing, to find comfort and to provide some type of hope to many of us who are still dealing with these difficult issues."

—*Bamby Salcedo, President and CEO of The TransLatin@ Coalition*

"I am humbled by this collection of letters. The authors of this collection are at times unflinching, proud, triumphant and brutally honest in their truths. Each letter is utterly personal; engaging with the text in this format draws the reader close inside quickly and I enjoyed this process immensely. Reading these letters, responding to the depths of what is shared within this book, I was struck with the same ideas, truths and lived experiences that trans people have shared with me after watching *FREE CeCe!* everywhere we went with the film. I am glad to see these voices lifted in such an indelible way here."

—*Jac Gares, filmmaker, producer of* FREE CeCe!

"*Written on the Body* is a much-needed story of violence against transgender and gender non-conforming people that is deeply needed. Not just for the community, but for everyone who wishes to understand the violence that trans people are facing. It's a story for us, by us, and this is the space where voices are needed most. Thank you for bring together so many narratives and creating a space for voices to be heard in a world that does not validate the experiences of trans folk."

—*KT Richardson, sexual and domestic violence prevention worker*

"*Written on the Body* speaks to me as I'm sure it will other readers. It gives voice and sheds light on a very important subject. One that isn't spoken about very much. Trans and gender non-conforming bodies. People just want us to hide our bodies and not address them. We get this message from the time that we're children and it stays with us. For some of us, it never goes away. These wonderful stories share real life experiences. Experiences that people like me never thought we would be able to share. The shame and humiliation around our own bodies. Hiding and pretending. The assaults, rape and abuse we suffer at the hands of others. Sometimes thinking we deserve this treatment because we don't fit in. Feeling voiceless and powerless. Living our lives for everyone else except ourselves, until we cannot take it anymore. *Written on the Body* helps break this silence around trans and gender non-conforming people. It helps to empower us and educate others. It's an excellent read and resource, and just good for the soul!"

—*Kylar Broadus, founder of Trans People of Color Coalition (TPOCC)*
and Transgender Legal Defense & Education Fund (TLDEF)

of related interest

To My Trans Sisters
Edited by Charlie Craggs
ISBN 978 1 78592 343 2
EISBN 978 1 78450 668 1

How to Understand Your Gender
A Practical Guide for Exploring Who You Are
Alex Iantaffi and Meg-John Barker
Foreword by S. Bear Bergman
ISBN 978 1 78592 746 1
EISBN 978 1 78450 517 2

Trans Voices
Becoming Who You Are
Declan Henry
Foreword by Professor Stephen Whittle, OBE
Afterword by Jane Fae
ISBN 978 1 78592 240 4
EISBN 978 1 78450 520 2

WRITTEN ON THE BODY

Letters from Trans and Non-Binary
Survivors of Sexual Assault
and Domestic Violence

Edited by Lexie Bean

*Foreword and additional pieces by Dean Spade, Nyala Moon,
Alex Valdes, Sawyer DeVuyst and Ieshai Bailey_*

Jessica Kingsley *Publishers*
London and Philadelphia

First published in 2018
by Jessica Kingsley Publishers
73 Collier Street
London N1 9BE, UK
and
400 Market Street, Suite 400
Philadelphia, PA 19106, USA

www.jkp.com

Library of Congress Cataloging in Publication Data
A CIP catalog record for this book is available from the Library of Congress

British Library Cataloguing in Publication Data
A CIP catalogue record for this book is available from the British Library

ISBN 978 1 78592 797 3
eISBN 978 1 78450 803 6

Printed and bound in Great Britain

These are the most used words in this book.

To those who wanted to write, but believed that they didn't have anything important to say, this is for you. To those who might find this book to be the closest thing they will ever have to community. To those who are not out; to those who are no longer with us; to everyone in between; to everyone who struggles with the word "enough."

CONTENTS

DEAR
YOU

WE ARE IN THIS TOGETHER

by Dean Spade

We are alone. We are connected and accompanied. These two truths return to me again and again in my own processes of healing from trauma.

On the one hand, I am the only person who will ever know or experience my internal experience. I am alone in it. I am uniquely positioned to observe and appreciate it. I am the person best qualified to care for myself. I am the person whose regard for my being and my body is the most important. Recovering from a culture of social control that requires us to attune to the expectations and opinions of others, this relationship to self is powerful to feel and appreciate.

On the other hand, no matter how abnormal, stigmatized and degraded we feel, we are not alone. We can hear our experiences echoed in the accounts of others. We can find connection, even across differences. Where human connections feel out of reach, we can connect to plants, animals and celestial bodies. We are accompanied. We are not alone.

This beautiful collection brought these two truths to me in new ways and deepened my experiences of them. The authors in this volume offer so much for relating with ourselves and feeling connected to others. How does anyone survive the violence and dehumanization that are routine conditions of existence in contemporary social and political arrangements? We survive by having brilliant bodies that hold, hide, express, contain, freeze, abandon, act out, and restrain. These poems and essays honor that exquisite labor and the scars it leaves.

These letters stir deep feelings and memories, and we can pay attention to what we need while reading. Maybe it means only reading a little at a time, or only reading when there is someone nearby for support. Maybe it means only reading at certain times of day, or sober, or after having eaten, or when well-rested. Maybe it means asking a trusted friend to read ahead and help us skip parts with content that would not be right for us right now. It is worth going slow and planning for support.

For gender rule-breakers, finding words and images about our bodies and sexuality that ring familiar is a matter of survival. We need different words, different images, different frames for understanding ourselves and our parts and reclaiming what is stolen by meanings that have been forced on us. We are projects of reinterpretation. This book is a gift to us from our siblings, generously sharing their hard-won meaning-making so that we might live with a new light, a new sensation, a new pulse running through our parts. Their wisdom and vulnerability offer a perspective from which we might regard our bodies again. The possibility of compassion for ourselves, of gratitude, maybe (conditional?) acceptance lives in these pages.

I love other trans and gender non-conforming people. I love your outfits, your self-fashioning, the way you spell your names. I love it when you change your name again and again. I love it when you break rules I did not even realize were there until I felt you free me. I love how you do not fit, how you expand what is possible, how you make room for each other and for me to imagine that we are allowed to exist. Where self-love feels inaccessible, reading others' accounts of their own navigation of shame, self-hatred, resistance, pleasure and healing makes new things possible for me. Seeing freedom where I feel rigidity and shame frees me. Witnessing others holding all the complexity of our survival inside brutal systems gives me relief and strength.

I am deeply grateful to these authors, and to their bodies, for keeping them moving toward integrity, connection, and aliveness. May this book support all of us to dismantle all the norms that strangle us and feel our deservingness to be alive in our bodies, alone and together.

FOREWORD

by Nyala Moon

L oving my body enough to start transitioning has led
me on an interesting path that no one planned for
me at birth. A path I didn't know would lead me to a few
hard moments, like being raped. A path that led me past
those hard moments into sweet ones, like finally feeling
comfortable enough to skinny dip with my friends. The
more I transitioned, the more I entered a space where I
received romantic interest from men. As a 19-year-old, I
didn't understand the potential dangers of this attention.
Truthfully, I was just happy to finally be noticed by guys
who I thought were attractive. That attention became
unsafe on a fun night with a guy of my dreams. He
became violent and raped me. He tried his best to claim
my body and my power for himself. And he did for some
time; it took me years to move on. But I healed myself and
restored ownership over my body. I eventually let go of the
blame I placed on myself for allowing myself to be in that
situation. It took a while for me to realize and truly believe
that I had a right to exist in my body, free from assault
and rape.

This body that is given to us is not only our own. They
are genetic tapestries of the past, your past; your mother's

smile, your father's height. When I was a young kid before puberty, it thrilled me when people would tell me I looked so much like Mr. Percy. I saw my grandfather as this all-powerful, all-knowing, giant figure. He was quick-talking, smooth-talking, always-talking kind of guy. Oh, how desperately did I want to be him. My grandfather was my father, he was the only father I had known. We loved playing chess, eating Snickers bars and having endless conversations. My birth father had died of AIDS shortly after I was born. I never knew him; I would hear stories about him. Family members would tell me that he was a quiet, stoic kind of guy, not like Mr. Percy. I didn't dwell on him. Because how could you miss someone you've never known, right?

I didn't think of my body in terms of my transness until puberty happened. It was the first day of school, and I brought my new Pokémon cards and Beyblades that I had gotten through an allowance system my grandparents had set up. I worked hard. I made sure the dishes were done after dinner and did many runs to Walmart. And after a lot of work, begging and convincing my grandparents to instead order online, I had finally had the perfect deck composed of half water and half psyche Pokémon. I was so sure that I had come to slay my classmates. I usually did; I was good at storytelling. However, not this time. Everyone was fixated on the cool group of boys. The leader of the boys stood in the middle of the circle of my elementary peers, flexing and showing off his newly hormone- and puberty-induced body. He had abs, muscles and a mustache. I was caught up in the wonders of tween attraction and horror that my body would sooner than later become like their bodies.

We had grown up learning survival skills and staying physically fit by doing military exercises. It was like a game to me. Mr. Percy was a man's man. He was a retired marine, who had reached the rank of E9, a master gunnery sergeant. As he often reminded us, he commanded and led thousands of men into war in Vietnam and Korea. Mr. Percy would run our family like a military family. Mr. Percy would never make me go as hard as my brother. I like to think he saw my transness, my womanhood, and decided not to go hard on me because of it. He never made me feel weird about being different, not once, even when my uncle came from California and tried to make a man out of me. My uncle's efforts were to no avail, but he made sure to shame me. He was the first person in my family who let me know I was a faggot. Other kids hinted at it by calling me gay and a sissy, but he confirmed it with his harsh words and disappointment in my lack of physical aptitude. As my brother and cousins started to develop this hyper-masculine body through my family's physical conditioning, I knew my fate was sealed. I didn't want my body to develop like theirs. I knew I was a woman and I wanted my body to develop like other girls my age. A part of me thought that somehow, someway, my body would just give me my fondest dreams. But it didn't.

I was 15 when I first discovered online that I could take hormones and medically transition my body into that of a woman's. I was filled with such happiness and joy. It was happening. I was becoming myself truly, even though I had to wait until I was 16. And wait I did! I remember sitting on the exam table as the doctor checked me out and gave me my first bottle of hormones. I had found the doctor through my friend, Nick, who was also transitioning. For the most part, I had to keep it secret. It's not safe in communities of color to be transgender and transition. Some people could tell I was changing, but my baggy gender-neutral clothes hid most of the changes. Some of my family started to notice that I was hiding something. My body started to change and I was proud of

it, but I was also confused by the changes. It wasn't until
Mr. Percy's funeral that my aunt made me cut my hair
and dress as a boy. I looked as if I should have been in a
hip-hop video: I had on Jordan sneakers two sizes too big,
with a matching sweater and Iceberg jeans. That's when I
developed a deeper shame in my body, even though I had
been taking hormones. Simply cutting my hair and being
made to wear boy clothes represented my whole identity
being locked up into the confines of my mind again. Much
later, I realized that I hadn't become like Mr. Percy or
the boys from my school. I had become myself. I knew I
couldn't be stopped.

Now when I look into the mirror, I do not hide, I do
not twist or curl my body. I see it fully for what it is and
what it has become. I feel a wholeness in my imperfection,
a wholeness that wasn't there until I made the choice to
reclaim my body. We trans folk have to reclaim ourselves,
we have to reclaim our bodies. The claiming of our bodies—
our bruised, broken and raped bodies—is a revolutionary
act. We reclaim because we have to for survival. If we don't,
we fade away, we die! At my granddad's funeral, as I saw
his dead body in the casket, I realized that I must take
ownership of my body. I had to choose life. I had to choose
my own life and body, which is what transgender and
gender nonconforming folks are doing by pushing past the
binary and forging their own path. Through all the pain
and trauma, we nonetheless persist!

In this beautiful anthology, you will read a collection
of transgender and gender nonconforming people
reclaiming their bodies through essays, poems, memories,
and testimonies of their own most personal and authentic
truth in the form of letters written to specific body parts.
Writing for this anthology has been a roller coaster of
emotions from neglect to shame, but also healing. We
all desperately need healing. The healing process can be

unlocked through nourishing acts like writing. Sometimes, I will be sitting in a coffee shop writing away and I'll start crying. And I'll think to myself, "Did I just write my pain down?" And I'll tell myself, "Yes I did!" By no means does writing completely heal the wounds, but it does stop the bleeding and sucks to walk through life with the hurting unnoticed. So I hope you read this and you are able to have a good cry at some random coffee shop. I fondly hope this helps with the bleeding.

DEAR YOU

by Alex Valdes and Lexie Bean

Dear Alex,

When do you feel safe?

With love,

Lex

* * *

Dear Lex,

I feel safe when the grey-blue early morning light peeks through my windows. I'm under too many covers, and I'm trying to match the soft breathing of the person lying next to me.

When did you find your trust again? Did you ever lose it?

With love,

Alex

* * *

Dear Alex,

I lost trust when I asked for help in the ways I knew how. I lost trust when he replied I was just following the cat into your room, but we all knew it was more complicated than that. I lost trust to the point where I became mute as a nine-year-old. I still struggle with this. I lost trust when he said he wanted to watch a movie, but we never got there. I lost trust when I lost count of the number of stories I have like this.

The other day my teacher pointed out that when I speak to support another, I project, I use my whole voice. When I speak for myself, I become small. The person next to me gave me a hug, and I couldn't feel a thing. I wish I could trust myself to be present enough to form a full sentence when someone asks me a question. I wish I could trust that my words can carry. I lose trust whenever I can't show up for myself, and I just crumble like an abandoned home.

There's nothing like feeling alone while lying next to somebody. That's when I'm at my loneliest. It makes it hard to trust myself, my sense of gravity, my breath.

I'm trying to find trust more than I lose it.

I trusted myself when I rolled on a vast wooden floor in Ohio, and got bruises on my own terms. I trusted myself whenever I remembered to water the plants. I trusted myself when I learned to cry when I feel it, instead of seven years later while standing in the aisle of a bookstore. I still also struggle with this. I trusted myself when I took off my roller skates, and my feet felt the solid Earth for the first time in hours. I trusted myself when I felt my own hip bones as I drifted to sleep.

What do you cover under covers? What was it like to take off your wig for the first time?

With love,

Lex

* * *

Dear Lex,

I shared a room with my sister (two years younger than me) up until college. Throughout our adolescence we would lie under the covers in each of our beds, across the room from one another. We would narrate and sort of play-act stories to one another for hours. (I naturally would play all the boy parts of course. Duh, it didn't make sense any other way.)

When I'm under covers, I'm building a hidden world, still. I'm no longer the physicality of this frightening body. I'm floating into the endless black sky and I'm warm; and sometimes I feel like I'm exploring the dreams or lives of other people as this pool of vapor.

My wigs were covers, too. I used to sleep in them because I couldn't bring myself to shed the character I'd developed. I wanted to only exist within a screen and under flashing lights and with images of burning houses projected over my skin. I was a femme fatale for too many people and always felt an emptiness growing.

There's a special kind of shame that comes with the removal of that fantasy. It's a violent act—tearing off the pins and the wig cap all in one motion—that forces your eyes closed. You open them, and you're left with a self that's more nude than you've ever been, and never ever enough for something that you can't feel with your fingers. Hair is so deeply personal and tragic.

My best friend shaved my head in the college dorm we
shared, between the beds we'd stumble home to at 4 am
to tell stories about the nights we'd had, at least one foot
always in fantasy.

"My hair is finally mine!" I remember telling her, rubbing
the stubble. My hair was mine, but only that much...that
half centimeter of length. For the first time in my life, I
forgave the child that was pressured into chemically
straightening away their curls.

Where is your voice when you can't find it in your breath?
When was the first time you fell in love with being alone?

With love,

Alex

* * *

Dear Alex,

I wrote a letter to my voice. It's in this book. When this
book is published, I can say that I can find it in these
pages. I'll keep it on my nightstand. I've never kept my
voice on my nightstand before. I wonder how different my
life would be if I had kept it so close when I was a kid.

I fell in love with being alone when I was seven. It was the
first time I was grounded. I pulled grass out of the ground
and cried out, "I'm a fairy!" I did not know at the time
that my new stepfather was obsessed with the lawn. I grew
up in Michigan suburbia, where people were obsessed
with cutting down all that grows in the wrong way. It
was then I decided it was better to be alone—for no one to
witness me. I savored my time in the basement, where I
used the space between my squatted knees as a shelter for
my plastic figurines. That's where the toys could talk, eat,
watch television, play in the imaginary backyard behind

my right foot. I knew from then on that my body could be shelter for what adults didn't see as alive.

Dear Alex, you talk often of the sky. What parts of you are the sky?

With love,

Lex

* * *

Dear Lex,

Where I grew up you almost never saw the stars. I'd stare out the window into the darkness, and meet most of my own reflection. Every once in a while, the white and red twinkle of an airplane would cut across my distorted face. I think I still look for my reflection in the sky.

The self I'd see in mirrors never made sense to me. For so long, it was like looking at a body resting underwater. If I focused hard enough, I could make out individual parts without a whole. I didn't know what parts of me were mine unless I painted them on. It's why I have such focus on my face and hands—the things I have creative control over. I'm trying to love this body for its existence, I'm trying to thank my legs for their strength to run in heels. Every week I'm more and more thankful for the pulled bit of flesh that takes a needle of testosterone.

I would live in the sky if I weren't afraid of heights. Maybe I would've seen my own face sooner if I weren't so afraid of myself.

I love that you turned your body to a shelter. That resonates. I think you're very much a home, and I wonder if you also see yourself that way. If we weren't reduced to our physical forms, what would your body be made of?

I hope this finds you at the right time, whatever that means.

With love,

Alex

* * *

Dear Alex,

I also couldn't see the stars from where I grew up, but I think I was a cloud in a past life and maybe I'll go back to that after this life. My body is where I'm living right now. I don't expect it to be able to protect whatever it's housing. Your letter did find me at the right time. It reminded me to look up, not as an emergency exit or escape, but as an extension of myself. I felt my neck crack in the motion. What patterns are you interrupting? Where can you feel the snaps and cracks of them the most?

With love,

Lex

* * *

Dear Lex,

I can't deny the weight of the world and its happenings at this time. I feel shameful that I chose this point, of all times, to medically transition. I hope these letters are a method of turning inward, of finding connective tissue within this community that needs so much. I hope these letters can heal ourselves and each other, make us stronger for a world that becomes more and more frightening by the minute.

I know that I'm being most honest with myself when I feel the sting of my old name being used. I feel my knuckles, my neck, my ribs, all cracking in harmony when I deny alcohol. I'm trying to interrupt the patterns that sabotage me; I'm trying to believe that I do not need these things anymore. I'm working toward believing that I am deserving of love when I'm sober. Growth is painful and exhausting.

Lex, what was the most recent thing you let go of in favor of yourself?

With love,

Alex

* * *

Dear Alex,

You inspire me. You are transitioning your body into a place where you can stay in a world that tells you that you can't. This is the perfect time to say yes to ourselves and all of our connective tissue within this community, no matter how fractured, how frightening.

When I first started working on this book, I was sat down in a room in the Trump Tower in SoHo, New York. They told me that I only think I am trans because I was raped. I know this thought, this intervention, had good intentions— they wanted me to heal from *something*. What they didn't know is that I'm trying to heal from what happened to me; I'm not trying to heal from who I am.

It's hard to let go of that day in the Tower. Some days it's harder to let go of than the years of rape. But I keep moving in favor of myself. I feel it more and more distant the more and more I talk with you.

I came to realize people who love me call me Lex, even though I had always introduced myself as Lexie or, on rare occasion, Alexandria. A year ago, around the same time as the sit-down, I introduced myself as Lex for the first and only time. It was to Sawyer, whose words are at the tail-end of this book. I told him I wanted to practice introducing myself as someone who is loved. It was my way of asking for help. It was my way of trusting someone on a similar journey to see me without explanation or stories to prove myself as real.

What are the small ways you ask for help?

With love,

Lex

* * *

Dear Lex,

You are more deserving of love than you can imagine, and I feel honored to have been trusted with your name. Thank you for your words—I read them just as an awful experience was unfolding in front of me. It's so easy to feel unseen in this body. I wish I could find my nine-year-old self and tell him that one day just simply existing in your honesty would be celebrated as courageous.

I'm easing into being more direct in asking for help, and I'm so grateful it's been met with such support. I'm still not great at it—sometimes I call people in the midst of a 3 am breakdown to apologize incessantly about calling at 3 am. Sometimes I livestream my crying on a secret Facebook profile, visible to a very select few. I call them makeup tutorials.

One of the most amazing things I've ever been told is, "I'll always pick up the phone."

I'm finding a lot of parallels between that online support and this anthology. I hope others find solace in that we are ever-healing, beautiful beings, with so much strength in these bones.

"You and I, we suffer." My tearful landlady held me in her 89-year-old hands as I pulled the last of my bags out of the house. "I want someone to love you for everything you are, not just someone to spend the night with," she said.

Lex, when did you last feel seen for all of the magic you're made of?

With love,

Alex

* * *

Dear Alex,

Would you like to process the awful experience you mentioned in your last letter? (If not through writing, maybe through a scream or a dance around your computer.)

One of the most amazing things I have been told is "You are here now" when I was caught in a flashback. She reminded me I was in Ottawa, Canada. She said it over and over because it can be so easy to forget. It's even easier to forget with a long history of choosing people who also forget; people who climb my bones, who make me nervous that they will leave if there are too many obstacles. Or maybe I would have gotten some sort of "Bad at College Certificate" for allowing my trauma to seep in when I am supposed to be fun and so alive. I didn't want to tell them that I didn't know where I was. People can take advantage of those who are lost; they could choose a destination on my behalf.

Last night while on the phone, a friend named Paul told me an amazing thing. I asked, "Are you afraid of me changing?" After a long pause, he said, "I think I'm afraid of me changing." This didn't necessarily make me feel seen, but as my teammate Jacob likes to say, "Transformation is always possible." I think that's where the magic is—the change.

I've given up on changing people's minds, but I want to invest in the miracle, the changing of hearts.

Last week I was on a couch in Oregon, and learned a song on the guitar for the first time. It's called "Dance, Dance, Dance" by Lykki Li. The chorus sings, "I was a dancer all along." I resonate with this. Finding a word can also feel like magic, just as learning a song can feel like a change of heart.

What word would you put for yourself? "I was a _____ all along."

With love,

Lex

* * *

Dear Lex,

I'm grateful I was able to process the awful sensation I referred to by getting my hair cut: literally shedding the weight of the day. I made friends with my barber, I've been thinking about him since. He shared a song he wrote with me and I've been thinking about what a lovely and vulnerable thing that is to do. I love this reference of hair and intimacy that we've made in our letters before.

If I had discovered sooner I was a musician all along, I would've saved myself a lot of self-doubt. I'm more than grateful for my dear friend Sean who placed a microphone, a looping pedal, and a reverb pedal in front of me and said, "All you have to do is mess around. You'll figure out what you like." There is nothing quite as powerful as a wall of harsh noise. I hope he knows how important he is to me.

Lex, what do you think you'll feel when this anthology is complete? Who is the first person you'll gift it to?

With love,

Alex

* * *

Dear Alex,

"All you have to do is mess around. You'll figure out what you like" is so dear. I think of gender the same way, a constant navigation and collaging of what I like. I appreciate that you let yourself be a lot of things at once. More than just words or parts, we are stories.

To be totally honest, when my last anthology of letters from domestic violence survivors was published, it took me years to be able to sit down and read it. I felt burdened by people who labeled the book as too heavy, but never took the time to read it. Since then, I've learned that nothing is heavier than silence.

This time will be different. I'm excited. I feel more breath at this point in my life. I feel the release more than the heavy. I'm not growing out my hair to make me feel more valuable to someone else. I'm not in hiding. I'm proud of myself for not buying a plane ticket to flee the country, just to feel safer in my sharing. And in sharing this, I've come to terms with the fact that I will continue to come out as many different words in the course of my life. That's why

I like letter writing. There's room for building, questions, and uncovering secrets I have even kept from myself.

Lisa Neumann and Heather Sedlacek, when you read this, know you are the first two people I'm gifting this book to. You know why, and I love you for it.

Alex, where do you keep the letters you never sent? Where did reading the letters that fill these pages send you?

Alex, when do you feel safe?

Thank you.

With love,

Lex

* * *

Dear Lex,

I wish I didn't know this was the last letter. I feel so grateful for this glimpse into your experiences and I'm so, so proud of you and what this book can do for so many others. I wonder if we'll peel back these pages, years later, with new eyes. I have a new trust in healing, and I have this anthology to thank for that.

I'm excited you're excited; so am I.

I've built this skin around so many unsent letters, resting in notebooks never finished. They live inside me until they live on a page. Some unsent letters can make you sick if they're stuck in your guts for too long. I'd much rather give them a home that I can then add to my own structure.

When I was writing these pages, I had to reconcile with a younger self. I had to find him, hold him, tell him I loved him. I had to promise him he had a future.

Being a trans survivor of assault is in a lot of ways being fearful of your own body. I needed these pages to remind me that I love myself, and that I am not the vicious ways I've been hurt. I had to reconcile my relationship with this physical world.

Safety is everything. That's what we continue to be told, and for good reason. This world is not welcoming for people like us, but that will never ever mean we're going away. I'm safe when I'm laughing. I'm safe when I'm untouchable—on that stage (or illegal basement venue) sharing what I've built with the audience. I'm safe in their "thank yous" and their "this made me feel things I wasn't ready for" in their "I understand you so much more now." I'm safe right here with you, miles away reading this.

You are so dear to me. Thank you.

With love,

Alex

THE
BODY

THE LETTERS

Dear Rib,

As the story goes, you were removed from Adam to create Eve. A piece, taken from man, to create woman. And men have been resenting the loss ever since.

In my body, however, you held firm and unwaveringly strong against large hands gripping you as the rest of my body was treated like an object, against baseballs thrown at you, against the collapse of your wards, my lungs and my heart.

During every panic attack, during every depressive episode, as my lungs and then my heart took turns shriveling, you protected them.

You protected them, and you protected me, as we were terrorized, but you are not without complications yourself.

Because you, my friend, are a remarkably gendered bone.

You made Eve, the woman who caused the Fall, whose flagrant female sexuality was too much for the perfect Eden.

But I don't want to be Eve. I want to be Lilith, Jewish mythology's feminist demon, created from the same dirt as Adam. Lilith didn't like Eden, didn't like Adam, didn't like prescribed femininity and the subservience it entailed. So she left. She left there, she left him, she left it all.

Now I navigate the leaving. I have neither Eden nor Adam to leave. But I have a name, and hair, and a role designated by my birth in this body. Now I leave them all.

Rib, you made Eve. You were strong enough to hold up against the large hands, the baseballs, and the misbehaviors of my heart and lungs. You were strong enough, once, to make an entire woman from a piece of another person.

Now, can you make an entire person from a piece of woman?

Dearest Skin,

Despite the art I have carved into you, you provide me with an impeccable memory.
I know of all of the places I've hurt and been hurt, and I won't forget them.

to my body-

i'm sorry that you became a battlefield.
neither of us ever wanted this, but
destiny is not easy to run from and
with every passing moment you are farther away from me.

to my eyes-
i am sorry the light was stolen from you.
that they covered the stained glass windows to our soul
with vantablack:
S V I S, blocking ninety-nine
point eight percent
of all light,
but like khatun i would rather you be struck blind than
bear witness
to the atrocities that will befall this body
in the name of survival.
in the name of a light bill.

to my hands-
you deserved so much more;
to be held with meaning like
you are more than just spare parts
made to be commodity sold in pieces.
you have spent so much of your life
tied toward one another but
you
are not bound to the needs of someone else.
so, do not grind your bones underfoot just
so some boy with a two dollar haircut
and chipped black nail polish can rise
and have a really good story to tell.

to my breath-
   i am sorry i lost you.
   come back.

to my blood vessels-
   carrying electric signals like a radio switcher
   you let me feel everything.
   for that i can't help
   but hate you.

to my mind-
   you kept me from everything,
   leaving
   only gaps in nights full of color and life. i thank you
   for pulling me away from here.

to the tendons in my heart-
   entropy is the second law of thermodynamics.
   the natural state of this universe is chaos.
   everything dies. i'm
   trying to think of a poetic way to tell you
   that your broken strings will never be repaired but rather
   become a chapel to all the times we've been used,
   but it's no use.
   a graveyard knows it's a graveyard because
   it's where things that have been forgotten
   come to disappear.
   i'm here.
   it hurts to be alone,
   believe me, i know.
   but i'll stay with you.
   we'll grow a meadow
   from the things we've tried to forget.

to my tongue-
   i thank you for never giving up the fight,
   even when im unable to put together a sentence.

the best is
when you continue to fool the people around me
who could not read a cry for help
if it were written into their hands like umbridge.
ever the deceiver.
you can repeat lies like scripture like,
i'm okay!
i just know
i'm going to be okay
because that is what i truly believe!

to my legs-
i promise the only time you will ever part
against my will again
is during exercise.

to my hair-
i will never cut you
just for the privilege of care.
you are worth more than the stains in someone else's bed.
you are sacred strands of goddess fabric
passed from the morrigan.
i am proud
to have someone pull you
even if i want them to stop.

to my nails-
dig until you draw blood
find the little ways to make him pay.

to my smile-
come back.

to my ears-
don't give up on me now.

to my feet-
keep running because
the worst is not over.

To the folds and flaps between my legs,

You make me uncomfortable.

Your shape confuses me and causes me to question who I am, what I am. You're a jigsaw puzzle piece that doesn't quite fit anywhere, but we manage to make it work.

We've always made it work.

I silently succumbed to your limits, always gentle and careful with my prodding. You make yourself scarce underneath your wealth of thick curly hair, hiding the form that feels like a betrayal. You remind me that it doesn't have to be a betrayal, that you are what I make you and you know that I'm never out to harm you.

But other people, they try to harm us. They're not so gentle in their prodding, nor do they respect the silent understanding we've forged. I hear that it's wrong that we don't touch each other or look at each other, that real love would entail both of these things. And people shame me for not pushing things inside of you.

They don't know our agreement: you hide your naked form to console me and I end the silicone war against you.

You know we're trans just as much as I do, and so objects being inserted into you feel terrifyingly foreign. You're not a vagina, you're not a vessel for man and his seed. And I will not take that away from you because someone tells me to. I'll let you live in what folks may see as blissful ignorance, in all your hairy glory and without the pressure of acknowledging your femininity. You don't want to be a vagina because you aren't one. And I would never force you to be one by using you in ways that force you to disassociate. You are a magical hairy pulsating sex machine, and one day we can sew up that hole. We can sew it up and we can forget it ever happened. And no one will hurt you ever again. I promise.

Our relationship really started after the assault, after I was forced to confront the ways in which and the reasons why my body was the way it was. I didn't realize just what you were trying to tell me until you were threatened: until the fear of being forced to be both a victim and a woman took over us in those 5–10 minutes I struggled to fight him off. I always saw you as a "work in progress." But I'm starting to think that perhaps it is I who is the work in progress. Maybe I always have been, and you've been perfectly imperfect all these years, saying the same thing over and over again. You always knew it, but it just took me a long time to really listen.

Physically, the space between my legs is you. No amount of pubic hair or careful maneuvering could change the fact that you exist. The folds decorating your depths feel deeply wrong, confusing even. So confusing that you couldn't stand to allow a tampon to be placed inside of you when I attempted such a feat at age 11.

But I see you now, I know what you are.

When I close my eyes, I can feel you as my dick between my legs in my hand. This is especially the case when I'm aroused. I can feel you hard and pulsating—and it's the most natural feeling in the world. The flesh you're in now is certainly entrapping, but an imagination is a lovely thing.

But you're endangered. Endangered by a world full of hate and by my heart, which is full of confusion and doubt about you.

I sometimes wonder if I want to erase you because we were assaulted. That is to say, what if I'm not really trans, but merely a cis female survivor of sexual assault? What if I only want to get rid of my vagina because of the vulnerability it represents? This is what my mom asks me, and the more she asks this, the more I wonder. The more I consider returning to a life of betraying your truth.

I wonder if I could go back in time and tell my abuser, "wait, stop, I'm really a man," would that have made a difference? Would he have hurt me, us, anyway, or even more so due to my dishonesty and gender identity? Or would he have said, "oops, my bad" and walked away from me? Is it right to want to shift rape culture away from me because I'm not a woman? Is it wrong to be confused about being subject to anti-female rhetoric from men while really being a man myself? Is it wrong that my gender identity truly feels more than besides the point when it comes to misogynistic actions and culture?

I want to stop assigning my politics, societal expectations and my fear of being problematic to my feelings and my body. To you, vagina. Is it okay if I call you something different, by the way? Perhaps "va-hoon?" I heard Ilana Glazer say that once, in Broad City I think, and immediately took a liking to the phrase. I hope you feel that it suits you.

Most of all, I hope you know that you're beautiful and worthy of love. Even if you don't look quite right. I am your ally and I'm always listening.

Love,

Dear Torso,

Did you know the body is a diary? It's written all its secrets underneath the skin. Sometimes my brain reminds me that if I just dig deep enough I could carve them out and get rid of them.

Other times, Torso, I wish people could just read you plainly. See the words you've braved (and spoken) and respond accordingly with a kindness usually reserved for grandmothers.

But this letter isn't a request to other people, Torso. It's to you.

You're too much. The days you are paunchy and exist too heavy for me to carry. The days you have curves when all I want is straightness. The days you have breasts when all I want is flatness. You, too, betray me Torso. Like all those placed on you before.

How could I be trans and survivor and femme and have this be a love letter? These identities are an admittance that my body is a battlefield, that I live in constant defeat.

How dare I feel intimate with you, Torso? Nothing has been won. Only conquered and forsaken.

Instead of closeness there lies the constant ache. Anxiety twisting ulcers into your core, growing where they don't belong. Serotonin receptors misfiring because they feel like they can, or they forget to feel at all. Nausea from this or the other illness settling in, deciding your comfort is inconsequential. How many have built a home of you without permission? I've lost count, but I know you keep track.

You, Torso, who bore the bruises. Above choked breathless, below entered and accosted. But you, Torso, you kept us together.

You with your insistence that each breath be taken. That these lungs in this chest expand to full capacity. How dare you demand that much space? Unbelievable, Torso, that with every fall you still rise. You have been beaten, Torso, so literally beaten by the girls who have loved you, and yet you stay defiant. Shoulders to hip bone you stay stoic, stay wanting, stay here. You have stayed with me, Torso. How could I be anything but grateful for that?

As broken, as untouchable, as unlovable, as incurable, as awkward curves as you are—you, torso, are the only one I can trust to hold me up.

Your other half,

Hey, you...

I feel self-conscious about this now that I've started writing. Oh well, never mind. I haven't really talked to you much, have I? I mean I've thought about you loads, and I've talked about you a lot, but. We haven't really talked yet, so it's about time.

Did you know that I coined a new term for how you came about? I think it's really cool, I call it Genital Upcycling Surgery... You used to be an outie, and now you're an innie, and way more functional and aesthetic. Okay, I don't mean functional like that, you know – I mean functional as compared to the dysfunctional we both felt when you were an outie. You make me happy, having you in my life, in my body, and I'm very grateful for that. I hope that you're way happier as an innie than as an outie too, I get the sense that you are, or that you would be if...

I'm sorry you hurt all the time. This was always a possibility, they warned me this was a possibility, though I didn't expect it to happen. It makes it hard for both of us, doesn't it? It's just confused nerves is what it is, but three years is a bit much, I know. I just want you to not be hurting, and to enjoy being yourself, and for me to be able to move on from being so medicalised, and maybe to be able to enjoy things we're both capable of enjoying that have a heavy pain-price until now. I want you to know that I've done my best to get us help with that, it's taken so long to jump through all the medical hoops to get to this point, and it's almost here. Next week, in fact. I really hope it helps us.

But this isn't what I really wanted to write to you about. I wanted to say sorry to you for something. It's not the kind of sorry that's an apology, so much, because it's not for something that was my fault – it's more the sorry you'd say if a friend told you they were suffering. Because this wasn't my fault, but it happened to you and to me, and I am sorry I wasn't able to stop it happening.

That person we were in a sexual relationship with, who had no boundaries, and who we love still...remember that night a few months after you were born, and they asked if they could touch you, and I said no...and then they did anyway? I'm so sorry about that.

You know about my bad past – some of it happened to you and me when you were a young outie, remember? You don't have to remember. What happened when we were small makes it very hard for me to set my own boundaries around body, you know – and this incident I'm talking about, I couldn't stop it happening in time because I froze, and I'm sorry for the effect that had on you, as well as on me. I know you cringe at the thought of someone else touching you, now, even though you also kind of want that to happen, with the right person(s) – and I know it's not just because you hurt all the time, but because you fear more hurt, and also fear being touched without your permission. I get that.

I want you to know good things came out of that thing happening. It led to me telling that person I wanted our relationship not to be sexual any more. Because I can't trust them to respect boundaries, and I and you deserve and need that. Even if you didn't hurt we'd deserve and need that. I learned something big that day about deserving better. I learned that I can't give consent, because if I can't say no then I can't say yes – and then

I learned to begin to say no. So maybe one day we can say yes, if it feels right with you, and with me. Let's keep talking about it.

Oh, and maybe you remember my oldest male friend? They're not my friend any more, did you know that? Because they blithely asked to see you after you were born (like they'd ask that of any other friend, they sure as hell never asked back when you were an outie), and then they got really angry when I explained they'd made me feel unsafe. So we're free from the threat of them (I never liked their anger, but didn't used to have the love to say no), and you've helped me become that more assertive person I'm becoming.

Because acknowledging that you needed to be born, and then making that happen, was the first truly assertive thing I did, so you were born out of new strength and love. It's a work-in-progress, this love and assertiveness thing. Just like it took me a while to let myself declare myself genderless (we non-binary people in our 50s are thin on the ground still, but I'm determined to be visible, to disprove all that "it's only a phase young folk go through" nonsense, we're everywhere and everyage). I'm telling you that because it doesn't affect how much you belong where you are in the world, and in my life (you should always have been there), and learning to be my truer self out loud is something you've played a vital and beautiful role in.

I think that's it for now. I really hope that soon we'll both stop being in so much pain, and can explore what the hell that's like, together as well as separately! I love you, I think you're beautiful <3

Dear Hair,

Oh, you have gotten me into so much trouble. When I was fifteen and I grew you longer and longer, it was so I could cut you off in a rush and donate you to Locks for Love. For years I'd heard—as people reached out and touched my hair—that you were beautiful, so thick and lovely, and someone would want to have you. I was used to self-sacrifice, so I was more than willing to cut all of you off and hand you over, even in the midst of my own nightmare.

I was eighty-five pounds at fifteen. "Anorexia nervosa," everyone said. I was rushed to the hospital. Dealt with therapists day in and out, who asked if my dad had ever been mean. Ever been...you know...too friendly.

I saw through them like I saw through my new bangs.

The correlation of sexual abuse and eating disorders was high. Even at fifteen, I knew that—because it was what my mom said. It was what my mom, who took away my dad and told me he was going to harm me, was convinced had happened. But it wasn't true. Not quite. I was used to giving up my body, but only through my hair, my hair, my hair, my hair. And only to her.

At ten, do you remember when I got a bad haircut and Mom flipped out? "She looks like a boy!" she said, lamenting my lost locks in thick handfuls.

Her words cut. It was the first time I realized that you, dear Hair, could signal something other than strength. When I left the eating disorder clinic, gaining weight and being a "good girl" for all the doctors, I dyed my hair. You became something I could control again, something that was going to be solely mine from now on. I became blond then blue then cherry and fire hydrant red.

And she brought me back into the eating disorder hallways. "She's rebelling," Mom told my therapist. "Too much is happening. And her hair—look at it! She cuts it herself now."

Eventually, I caved. I tried to give up my hair and strength like Samson. If my thoughts were bad, like everyone told me they were, I wanted to get them at the root. I yanked you out, piece by piece, giving myself up in shards, expecting redemption.

But you came back.

Hair, you stood strong. And I decided to stand strong with you. Everyone could have my body; take it away bit by bit by bit by bit. But you were permanent. Each time I cut you and fucked up the bangs, you were forgiving. You grew. I grew. And when I shaved my head in Mom's kitchen, changing my name the next week, it felt like a new life had started.

I was not the person with anorexia nervosa, not the same name on the wristband. My body had already gone through so many iterations; so many sizes and hormones and fucks and bruises. You, Hair, were the same but brand new. You were the same but brand new. The guiding light, the thing that always grew even at my thinnest. The thing that always came back with forgiveness, proving to me that my thoughts were never wrong.

I was never wrong.

I'm sorry, Hair. I've given you a bad rap. You were there to keep me warm when I was skinny, my scarf for a perpetual winter. And when I wanted to be a boy, to be queer, to be something other than the DFAB person everyone told me I was, you allowed me to shape you into new styles signalling new names. Now I could do what I wanted with you, whatever colour or length or style. And through your inches and your iterations, I also got my body back.

My thoughts grow from the crown chakra and flow down to my feet. I don't keep my hair long anymore, but I also know I don't need to sacrifice myself, any part of me, in order to keep anyone else loving me. I am enough; three inches is enough. So thank you, Hair. You never got me into trouble. You always, like the sweetest fairytale, pulled my tangled thoughts out.

To the one hair that grows out of my cheek,

"It's time you pluck that out. People will make fun of you for it." This was the only fourth-grade advice I remember from my mother. I borrowed her make-up mirror to observe myself under the harsh light, and my eyes widened at your thickness. Nothing felt more true.

I pulled on you like a weed, your tip darker than the rest. It was a relief, the idea of being better after a simple action at your expense. I wanted your absence to heal me, to tell me that I could stay in this body without a fence. Even on days they told me at school that my ears were too big, I blamed it on you. "Contain yourself," I scolded you as I again leaned into the make-up mirror. I blamed you for making their eyes notice me. How could I let you resurface? You crawled up insistently through the moles of my face labeled as sun-damage. I blamed myself, too.

Everything that they said was true.

After all, the only way to make a wish on a dandelion was by blowing all of the hairs away. The further away they went, the more likely the dream would come true. By the end of the fourth grade, I stopped making wishes altogether, too distracted by the brown residue on my palm from the stems that maybe never wanted to be plucked. Teachers decided to ban dandelion bouquets from the classroom that year; they said leaving the weeds to the grounds-keeper was a part of growing up. In the fifth grade I made a list of every part of myself I would ban from my body. You, that single hair sprouting from my cheek, were third from the top.

It took me fifteen years to realize that a weed is only a
word, a living thing made ugly. The truth is a weed is one
that grows despite everything, whose roots threaten the
ecosystem of someone else's plan. You marked my impurity,
sprouting instead of everything else that was supposed
to grow: my breasts, my hips, my mascaraed eyelashes.
My mother wanted you to hide so the rest of us could
bloom into a beauty worthy of picking and taking home to
decorate the kitchen table.

—

But you always grew back, always thicker than the
time before. In a frenzy I pulled you out again. Just as I
constantly pulled out the passing thoughts of:

he shouldn't be here, I am a boy,
I want seconds, I love her,
that part of me that leaves whenever I wear a bra,
I want thirds, he shouldn't be here in my bed,
I'm in love with her, I am a growing boy,
Where is God?

Rip you out, rip you out. Blow you away. Anything but that,
the pain of being consistently out of place. Do something.
She would say, "Do something. You're such a pretty girl,
why would you let yourself go?"

—

My truths became weeds climbing out of the suburban
sidewalk cracks. Mow you down, quick, mow it down, look
nice for the neighbors. Please, don't make fun of me, but
we are so good at the lie.

I felt the dread of holding just one more hair of space.

I felt that if I had let you grow, I would start seeing myself
in the mirror as questioning and whole. I pull you out on

days I tried to make my growing pretty for someone else. The "it's time to be safe in your body," the "it's time to take care of yourself" running rampant until, pluck. I leave you in on days I do not leave the house. However, on days I truly feel "it's time to be safe in your body," "it's time to take care of yourself," I can imagine you growing into an entire field. You, no longer alone, spread across my cheek and towards my mouth, outlining the place where most of my secrets live.

What they don't want you to know is that weeds can nourish the body. In some places, people cook dandelions, sip tea brewed with what my mother stepped on. Plant the rejects on their windowsills on purpose. There are people who could be happier taking in the morning sun just because you are there. What they don't want you to know is that they often pull weeds because they're just afraid to see what they could grow into. Afraid of their human capacity to destroy something that they were capable of loving. There is a reason children don't blow all the dandelion hairs away when making a bouquet to give to someone they love.

What they don't know is that I have never cut you off by the root. You're a secret garden, terrifying and beautiful, here even when you're gone.

With love,

To my hands:

I see my mother in you every day. You are her gentle wrapping of veins across delicate bones. But her knuckles are perfectly aligned, her fingertips follow through in a gestural sway.

The fourth metacarpal on your right was snapped under the weight of a man's knee when you were trying desperately to be physically strong and tough in a space where they called you "the girl in the pit" and you hated it so much and all the boys wearing the same fucking hat and shorts swinging and punching the air in this short-sighted vision of masculinity. Your own fists could never be hammers and you knew but you tried anyway and your crooked knuckles will always speak this for you.

You are calloused and scarred because there is something about being devoted to physical carelessness that excites you.

I remember the first time you relaxed in the palm of another. "We have the same hands!" the nail technician said, but it wasn't true. She had my mother's hands. The same mother that said "Never forget what they did to us, stay angry" with the softest touch it was a sign I know it was when you emerged tipped with long red claws. It was a promise to be a new weapon.

I am so proud that you love it when people call you frightening, alien-like. The truth is you are terrifying. You are harsh femme. You are a new masculine that people won't understand for a long time but that's okay because until they do you'll still catch their eye and all attention is good attention unless of course it's the 10 minute walk home at 2 am that reminds you of how you can't close yourselves into fists anymore.

And maybe one day someone will extend your fingers apart, count every scar like a blessing, and call you beautiful for being exactly where you are in that moment.

Thank you for being the only part of me that ever made sense. I love you.

Dear Mind,

A few nights ago, we sat in the receiving room at the JPS psych ward, and we were vindicated.

After a phone call made to our religious grandparents proclaiming we were so sick of the poverty we'd experienced and wanted to die since our divorce—we were cuffed and placed in the back of a police car once again. But this time it was very, very different.

We were in the most healthy brain space we'd ever been in our life. Our roommate, who has actually had contact with us for the last ten years, vouched for us. We were proclaimed, for the most part, healthy besides maybe a need for optional sliding-scale counseling. We were fed sandwiches.

We were told we were okay, even with our dysphoria, even with our imperfection.

After our rough ride—we were happy for a smooth one and a cab ride home.

We did yoga, wrote poetry and drew intricate flowers as two psychiatrists asked us questions and couldn't see what was wrong.

We looked out the window at all the shimmering lights in Downtown Fort Worth and the old Jewish graveyard and realized that the barbarism and lockdowns we experienced on military wards and in Alexandria, Louisiana wasn't everywhere. In this place, it was as dead as the families who lived their lives and rested peacefully in the night.

We were done howling like Alan, and we began to slowly form a language of our own. Sometimes it was fits and starts. It was often gritty, but it belongs to us, and when we speak and find the truth it sets us free.

This ward proudly displayed a patient's bill of rights instead of a trite inspirational quote by St. Exupéry. It said dysphoria and marginalization were tough, but you could be tougher. It said the world can be wrong—but that doesn't mean there is something wrong with you.

For my mouth:

May you never soften for anyone that demands it.

You were never made to be small and silent. Look at you. Dare to reveal the mountains of teeth that fill your width.

I wrote several letters to you, most of them were pitiful and wanting, but you were not made of should'ves and could'ves and I'm so so sorrys. You carry the bones of your ancestors in your gums and they're the ones you call on when people stop you to ask, "What are you?" But not listening, never listening, when that same mouth says no. Those people don't look for the silence when you can't say no because you're afraid and want so much to be held in someone's hands like a pebble smoothed by the waves.

You are bigger and bigger still, and when the microphone smears your lipstick make sure they hear every single word that's screaming from the lips they said were too big.

You are how I found my way back to myself. I love you.

"A Thank You, with Apologies"

To my eyes, for all of they've seen, and all I hope they see,

You've been my constant companions, my first friends in this world and the last ones I'll ever have.

And I still don't know whether to thank you, or apologize to you.

You saw me born, as a doctor used his own eyes to misjudge who I was and who I would be. A designation, a single "M," that would shape my life in so many ways that I never wanted.

You saw me grow up at the feet of my grandmother, helping her cook every day. She now resents herself for that, thinking it's what made me what she considers abhorrent.

You saw me introduced to my new father at age 5, my mother's hope for a happier life. I don't think she ever got her wish.

You saw me become older, and have the first glimpses of what it meant to be myself. I called myself Julia back then, a name I moved past until later.

You saw my father's reaction to Julia, the abuse he heaped upon me as his "son" tried desperately to become his daughter. The emotional scars may be invisible, but you saw everything that formed them.

You saw me move away at 17 to college in a far-off state, running as far away as possible. Much like my mother, I hoped for a better life. And I, too, don't think I ever found it. Certainly not the way I hoped.

You saw me meet the woman who would become my wife. It was over sushi, and I was lost and wandering. Little did I know that wandering would continue, and yet the destination would be even worse.

You saw that same woman brutally attack me over and over because of Julia. I closed you to protect you from it. I'm sorry that I couldn't protect you forever and that you'd eventually see the bruises.

You saw me forced out of that relationship, on the night before Thanksgiving. I couldn't help but fill you up with tears, as the street became our home.

You saw me find temporary shelter, then move into a meaningless job that never made me happy. We were both dead, you and I, for so long. I'm sorry I didn't revive us sooner.

You saw me realize why Julia had been there so long, and what needed to happen. The fear as I came out to someone for the first time. The terror and joy I felt the first day I went to work in that horrible blouse and skirt combination.

You saw the world get instantly brighter with that first small blue pill, the estrogen that had been missing for so long. I still remember clearly how that darkness just suddenly lifted that day. You were finally fully there with me, the way it was always meant to be.

You saw me stand in front of a judge that day in September and cast aside the identity that had been imposed on me. I didn't call myself Julia any more, but I'd finally become myself, through a single sheet of paper.

You saw that darkness come back, though, because I made a mistake. He told me that his family could never know about me, that they would never understand me or accept me. And yet I still invited him into my home.

You saw him betray my trust. I just wanted a physical and emotional connection with someone. And he took advantage of that, deceiving me and forcing himself onto me. And again, I closed my eyes to protect you.

You saw me with that shotgun in my mouth, crying because I didn't know what to do. But someone else's eyes saw me, and stopped me from making another horrible mistake. I don't know how I'll ever be able to repay her.

But through this all, there's still more that I hope you'll see.

A few days from now, you'll see me awake from the first surgery that helps me become the person I'm meant to be. They'll cut away a part of me, and yet I'll become more whole.

Later, you'll see me complete the process of transformation. I'll finally look into the mirror along with you and see who I know myself to be, completely.

Someday, I'll find the person who erases all of the pain we've experienced together. The emotional scars, the bruises, the heavy weight on me, will be melted away as you look into their eyes.

And in the end, many years from now, as I take my final leave of you, I hope that you see joy instead of fear, a life finally lived with happiness. I can think of no better gift to give to you, and for you to give to me.

I still don't know whether to apologize or thank you.

But thank you. And I'm sorry.

People You May Know

After *Kevin Kantor*

To My Body,

When my abuser showed up under the people you may
know tab on Facebook
I could feel my heart drop into my stomach like the rock
he had turned it into
I looked down to my stomach apologetically
As my mind raced laps around itself and I played it back in
my head
It had been over a year since I had blocked him from my
life
It had been over a year since I had seen a picture of him
It had been over a year

I can't help myself
My hand moves over the mouse
My fingers push down
Click
A new profile picture
The hair he had grown since we started dating is now
shaved to his scalp
Nothing for someone to grab onto or pull when he pins
them down to the ground
Nothing for someone to use to defend themselves when he
is yelling into their face as he slams their
head into the floor
Over
And over
I can't stop my hands from shaking

Click
He took his lip ring out
Click
He's wearing my hat

Click
I miss that dog

Click
Click
Click

I look down at my body
I look at all of the recovery that has taken place
The bruises now long gone
The bones now buried by the weight I never could put on
And my body begins to shift
Suddenly I see my flaws more clearly
My stomach suddenly looks larger
My ribs buried deep inside start aching
Hiding from the world that used to be apart of
The man who
Bruised them
I hear his voice in my head again
All those years of complaints and criticisms
All those years of avoiding meals
Avoiding judging stares
Avoiding the concern that others had for me and my body

I look at my closet
At the clothes labeled "girl" that he hated
At the dresses hanging
At the wigs on their stands
All of the things he hated
All of the things that he said he would leave me for

Drag was an escape
A performance
Someone happy
But it was an unattainable goal
Those clothes were a fetish
Those clothes got him off
A trap
Trapped
The word echoed in my head again and again
Why won't you wear that for me?
He keeps asking
Because all you want to do is fuck me
And not let me be me
I am not your fetish
This body is not yours to fuck
And use
And abuse
This body is mine
My identity is mine
Not yours

I look back at my stomach and sigh
Where ribs once stuck out I see a layer of fat
My ribs now covered by the stack of books and ripped
pages of ink
I look at my legs
At the hair that is slowly growing
Shadowed by another tattoo wrapping its branches and
roots around me
I used this ink to help me
A tool of recovery to place a bandaid over parts of my body
that I hated

I pull out a pair of jeans that fit
Maybe just a little too tight
Feel the fabric over my thighs as I close my eyes

Smiling as I think about how right it feels
A tight tank top covers my chest
Make-up adorns my face
The mirror looks back at me
Beaming
There they are.

There I am.
Content.

Dear Eyes,

You've seen him, better than any other part of me, be so kind and so gentle and so loving. You've looked into his eyes and seen so much love for me.

You've seen him. You know he's not as strong as I am.

You also saw him hit me. You saw him laying in my bed and for a minute taking out his frustrations on me. You saw him continue to lay there, no obvious regard for the pain he had just inflicted on someone he claimed to love.

I know you hate to cry, that you don't like to feel unmanly. But I understand why you needed to cry so hard that night. And I want you to know it doesn't make you unmanly. You had had so many conversations with his eyes and you trusted him. Things had been hard between us, but I had trusted him too. I didn't expect to feel so hurt and betrayed and confused by him.

And the next day he wouldn't even look at you and you felt so guilty yet you felt manipulated too. You cried again and it all just felt bad, bad about him and bad about me. Later his eyes tried to tell you how sorry he was, but you didn't trust him because you had seen them so full of anger and aggression. And months later when I tried to bring it up once, his eyes flashed so full of anger at you and you had to see that directed at you again.

You've seen so much that hurt us, but I just didn't want to believe it all was real because I loved him so much. You were the eyewitness to all my worst moments after his betrayal too. I hadn't felt good about myself before the incident, but it just got worse. You were the only witness to my ensuing violence against my own body in my worst times of feeling lonely and worthless. It's not that I think that's his fault since it was my hand that held the razor blade, but also he made me feel just so worthless. The looks he gave you when I wouldn't cuddle or admitted I didn't feel like I could trust him were almost as painful as the day he hit me.

I know I should have saved you the tears by not going back to him the next week, even though I still loved him. I know I should have taken time away, so you didn't have to see him and see the replay of his aggression until you had at least stopped crying. And for that I am sorry.

Love always,

a kid who's just trying to move forward in his life

jupiter (a letter to my chest)

inhale.

my feelings about my body are like moons – they cycle,
changing shape as they wax and wane, grow light or
weary

sometimes they eclipse everything

but you have always been my jupiter – constant, heavy,
a large thud of muscle and fat,
an undeniable reminder of your own existence.

it isn't fair, I know;
you aren't the place where where he broke in
and yet you hold onto all of those memories,
clutch them tight, press them
into blood and skin

I don't feel heavy in the parts that were intruded
because they feel so hidden, tucked away inside myself,
and because I have made them hidden, clenched the
memories so tight
                that to remember them, now,
to unclench,
would be too much. it would break the dam,
it would loosen a boulder and start an avalanche,
send cracks of thunder and dust into the sky

but you know all about that, jupiter
named for the god of sky and thunder,
you are not afraid to be loud.
to take up space. to assert yourself
                into being.

you are brash and heavy in the world –
you are the thing that marks me, immediately, as 'female';
when all other signs point to indeterminacy.
you are the thing that sits, heavy, on my self
impossibly, irrefutability,
apparent.

I have gone through the world trying not to be noticed.

jupiter, I have spent so much of my life thinking of you
as a problem
wondering if pushing you down, removing you, making
you concave
                would make it easier to be invisible

but the feelings I have housed in your dense flesh
                are not just of you
;
you have worn them proudly, like armor,

you have protected me, all of these years,
from remembering his hands and his smell and his laugh
as he broke in.

                in offering yourself as a place to remember,
as a site of sacrifice,
you have given me permission to heal.

the romans swore to you, made you their oath-keeper,

                their witness.

Dear Feet,

Tuck yourself in beneath the Peter Rabbit quilt, toes
pointed out like a ballerina.

Moonlight warps the quilt into snails and lizards. A hairy
hand holding a neon carrot forces a hard, blunt tip into a
bunny mouth. Shimmy out the top of the quilt and put one
of you before the other. Careful not to let the Monopoly
shoe bring you to heel. Step into the dark bathroom,
lightswitch too high for me to reach. Slug slime oozes
between your crying-wee-wee-wee toes, sticking you to
the spot. Jasmine vine slips through the window to twine
around your ankles. No escape.

When Mom floods the yard because she's too drunk to turn
off the hose, wade into the swamp. Simon-Says-tiny-steps
sludge layers mud on your soles. Drag yourselves. In June,
put a toe in Sespe Creek. Fiddle with pebbles the adobe of
dry bougainvillea, burnt sage, and crushed ochre. Let fish
investigate your fissures. Jump in first. Hop boulder to
boulder. Sun yourself beside Everlasting and mallow.

Two left yous during a year of first love. Sink into beds of
redwood needles. Scuff mossy stone steps to a fairy cabin.
My girlfriend proposes. Get cold. You don't have ears,
so you're swept off. Whisky breath a numb weight from
which I couldn't escape with mere words. I choked on "No."
Put yourself down. It's raining. Get wet. Slide down the
paperwhite-lined driveway. Stumble along the shoulder
of no-sidewalk Highway 9. Hold steady at the pay phone
outside of St. Vincent de Paul. Kick me til I say, "I dug in
my heels and left."

Angel ankles. Every direction is elsewhere.

Hey Feet,

Our time together has been great. I'm happy to have
had you along for the ride my entire life. Scratch that,
in fact, you have been my ride my entire life. You've
been my most reliable form of transportation and most
definite feature that I share with my father. You know:
exceptionally long second toes, strong and balanced
arches. Remember when I was a little league baseball
player and had to squeeze you into those cleats with
the fancy leather flap on top? And how that aggressive
pitcher that all the players feared pitched that ball right
into my back and, even though I was winded, I smiled
and pretended all was fine because I had become a pro at
pretending that violent blows didn't affect me. It was you,
my cleated kid feet, that proudly trotted to first base and
eventually ran and stole second. You helped me to be fast!
And still do! The speed helps me get out of situations like
the one I found myself in 2 weeks ago when I was cornered
into the bottom floor of an abandoned brownstone and
made to suck dick or else pay the consequence of even
more violence. It was you, curious feet, that got my stupid
ass into that mess and it was your swiftness that got me
out after I waited for the perfect moment to save myself
from further violation.

When your toes are painted with pretty colors and I look
down and am reminded how art can live on my body I
feel special and proud—like I am a walking canvas. And if
I'm not feeling good about my gender because I'm afraid
of someone on the street attacking me or a small child
wondering aloud about why there's nail polish on my
toes sometimes not having nail polish on makes me more

relaxed because, in my head, it means that people won't be as hateful to me for expressing who I am. Or who I want to be.

But here's what I love about you, feeties. Once there's music playing, on the subway, in the club, on the streets, in the woods, you know what to do! You know how to move, without asking silly questions like, "Is this appropriate?" You just want to live and move and be wild and free. And that's my soul! If the stomach is the way to a man's heart, maybe the feet are the way to a dancing queer's soul.

Much love TOE you,

Dear asshole,

Three things. Unrelated. Sort of.

One, a month ago. I followed through on a two-year-old
threat and made a bunch of friends go to Coney Island for
a minor league baseball game. We drank beer and watched
the fireworks and raced around the bases and wound up
up to our calves in the Atlantic, the water numbing my
legs right up to the tattoo about my old name. I told them
that I wanted to get a tramp stamp, but I didn't know what
of. We went through spaceships and sea creatures and
patterns and then one of them said *how about a ghost* and I
made them all stop thinking because it was done.

Two, seven years ago. I graduated high school a year early
and got into a summer playwriting program. He was
twenty six and creeped out by how young I was. I promised
him the age of consent in New York State was seventeen.
He tried to stick his finger up my asshole; I pushed his
hand away. Later, we smoked weed, him for the millionth
time and me for one of the first. He stuck his finger up my
asshole. He lived in his grandmother's basement and told
me that when I was his age, I would be living much better
than he was. (He was right.) He told me that we should be
talking about sex, and how did I feel about his finger up
my asshole. I said it was fine, but I didn't mean it. He told
me that when he touched my buzzcut it felt like kissing
a boy.

Three, three years ago. I was living in a studio half a mile
outside Boston with a dude I thought was forever. He
wanted to top me for anal. He took my no as gospel, but
he did want to talk about it, and I wanted to talk about it

with him. I wondered out loud if I didn't want to because my asshole was haunted. He told me bottoming felt great and he really thought I'd like it. I wondered, silently, if anal wasn't for me at all, or if I wasn't really into topping him because of my gender shame. I told him that if he answered three riddles, I would let him top me. He spent the rest of the summer diligently asking yes or no questions. I refused to give him hints. By the time he got the last one, my depressive episode had ramped up, and I could barely drive, let alone fuck. He moved to California and took our dick with him.

I'm gonna get the tattoo at this shit shop in the East Village. They don't do great work, but I like it there. I might take the friend who came up with the ghost idea, but I might go alone. I like how tattoos feel, physically, and that liking makes me feel butch. I imagine it will hurt more than my others. I imagine I'll be embarrassed when I say that I'd like the ghost's tail to go all the way down to my asscrack. I imagine I'll do it anyway. I imagine myself at Coney Island next summer, those same friends by my side, my right scar red and raised and the left one totally faded because my insurance wouldn't cover a better surgeon, my ghost rising like a fairy princess mythic queen out of my sale rack H&M bathing suit.

Love,

The rest of me.

The following Poem written about my new body part: a source of wonder and pleasure.

Hello

Now I am real, the real me
No more the boy – the man
A new body
Approved of – by my mind
Wanted for ever
Beautiful bits, Squishy
Womanly bits for sure
So proud

Surprise
Where have you been?
Boobs not big, not small
Enough to fill a bra
Did I think one day?
My prayers would ever
Be answered – at all

How could I
Boys don't get Boobs
Right!

Excited with this new body
Experiences never known
Ignored the world and all its opinions
No suicide for me –

Thankfully

When asked
Why I had changed
It was the Hormones
What did it your Honour
I laughingly replied

Changed my body to a girl's
And Girls do – What
Have boobs
Wonderful boobs
Soft and round with nipples
A joy to behold
What Now!
This is me ecstatic – Happy at last

The following Poem written
about the body part I once
had: the source of considerable
pain and embarrassment.

To my penis,

At times – You gave me pleasure
A thing to play with – When I was bored
A part of me I did not understand
And then I did

Always present – I did not get you
My mind told me – You should not be there
But you were – So insistent
On getting – Your way

You confused me with your presence
I began to hate you
You never gave up
Always there – Always demanding attention

You're really ugly – A meaningless growth
On my young body – You have no place
But my – How strong you are
To the most innocent of my thoughts

You're always there

Damn you

And then it happened
You conspired with another – You deceived me to get your
way

The pleasure short-lived
The consequences forever undeniable Not once, but twice
you committed me
How I hate you

You do not belong – You do not define me
Never – You have to go
Discarded, so I can be real
The real me – Without you

A mind, stronger now – and older
Tells me it's time – You did your best
Thanks, but no thanks
I am woman – I know for sure

I've always known
You don't belong
You will be removed
Goodbye – Forever – Gone!

I.

Dear You-Who-Must-Not-Be-Loved,

I shouldn't have to write to you. I hate feeling like I do. It's
so fucking obvious, you know? I could be writing about
all the other body parts, the less over-hyped ones: Like
my hands. I should be writing about my hands, so quick
and clever. Hands that danced the piano from the age
of four, that still type poetry like they're making music,
fingers that have learned painstakingly over time to grasp
and hold and hit and heal and let go. My hands that are a
novel unto themselves.

Or I could be writing about my legs and feet. The parts that
have carried me so, so far, that knew instinctively how to
sway and sashay in high heels at twenty years old despite
a lifetime of being forbidden. The parts that know how to
run like the West Coast rain, that have saved me over and
over again.

I want to write about my sweet new breasts, swelling like
the buds of perfume-scented carnivorous lilies that only
bloom in the night.

And yet here I am, writing to you. It's stupid. It's cliché.
It's hackneyed and it's been done; it actually feels kind
of Hollywood and not in the good way. More like in the
cis-man-playing-a-trans-woman-for-an-Oscarbait-
movie kind of way. It feels like doing something for the
wrong kind of attention. Again.

Sometimes I feel like I should have gotten rid of you a
long time ago. I have friends who've done it – other trans
girls, braver ones. I have friends who are planning on
doing it. I know little trans girls, thirteen years old, who
are planning to get it: *The Surgery*. And maybe if I had been

stronger, luckier, more determined ten years ago when I first came out, then maybe everything would be different now. But I didn't. And it's not.

You never really had a chance, did you? You always get the bad rap, there is an evil story that rides inside you. And so in me. There you were, when I was born. It's a boy, the doctor said: your most grievous fault. There you were, in the bath when I was four. I touched you, and Dad smacked me. It's dirty, he said. I thought you were supposed to wash things that were dirty.

There you were, hidden in my jeans, in college when the professor in my Women's Studies class explained that *phallogocentrism* means that everything in society is organized around the sanctity of the penis and then looked meaningfully at me.

And there you were, betraying me, every time I was naked. Every time I had sex. Every time I was with a boy and he thought that the fact that I had you instead of a vagina meant he could do anything he felt like doing: Experiment. Use force. Laugh. Treat me like a weird species of undiscovered animal, except that undiscovered animals are considered rare and precious to science and trans girls are considered freaks. Whenever trans girls say that in public, some cisgender woman inevitably says, *they treat us like that too*. Trans girls know: *Not like this.*

Society often doesn't believe cis women when they say they have been raped. Society, even (and sometimes especially) feminist society, doesn't believe that trans femmes can be raped. To society, we are the rapists, because we carry or used to carry you between our legs from the day we were born.

They say that we are the ones who "trick" or "trap" poor hapless cis men into getting into bed with us. (Never mind that cis men kill and target us for violence at disproportionately high rates.) That we are forcing cis lesbians to accept sex with trans partners they don't want. (Right, because *trans women* are to blame for the oppression of cisgender lesbians.) That we lurk in public washrooms, just waiting molest little girls. (The people who are most in danger in public washrooms? Trans women.)

They say that the very shape of our bodies is "triggering" to other sexual assault survivors (read: cis women), because you are a dangerous weapon and the root of all sexual abuse. Patriarchy means that cis women are identified with blame or victimhood or survival, transmisogyny means that trans girls are identified with violence.

And every time I think or write about what happened to me, there you are, like a machine gun tucked between my thighs.

It's not fair.

I hate writing about this. I hate talking and thinking about it. I will not give details. I want the memories locked in an unmarked box under the sea. I want to never hear about it or be asked questions about it, ever again. And then maybe someday, I could write about you in a way that's different. Maybe I could write about you in a way that doesn't tell the story that everyone expects to hear about how I hate you.

And what I want to tell you, on that day, is that I know that it's *not your fault*. None of it. You were not to blame.

Maybe I could write about how when I was little, everyone told me you were bad and dirty and full of evil things, but I always knew it wasn't true. Maybe I could write about how I discovered that you could bloom with pleasure, like a flower in a secret garden in the middle of the night when no one was watching. How everyone told me that having you meant I was a boy, but I knew that wasn't true either. How they told me I had to get rid of you in order to be loved by anyone, to be seen and held and loved as woman, but this, too, turned out to be a lie.

Maybe I could write about those things.

Love,

Dear Heart,

It's hard work, letting someone in. But you've done it. You've let one person get so close to your heart, someone you feel really deserves it. I know sometimes you're hard on yourself for not having more people in that warm and incredibly close space of yours, pushed snugly in the area between your beating heart and your ribs. Instead, congratulate yourself for having gotten this far.

It's in your nature to protect your heart from others, anyway.

You've been hurt. You've been injured by what sometimes feels like centuries of abuse. You felt heavy when the doctor asked us, "have you ever experienced physical, verbal or sexual abuse?" and I answered, "all of the above."

In the midst of all the trauma, you were left in pieces and with a deep contempt and mistrust for men. Men that have done nothing but yelled at you, humiliated you, shamed you, gaslighted you, harassed you, assaulted you and silenced you.

I promise I won't get mad at you anymore for not healing fast enough. I'll no longer curse you on the way out of the grocery store after you verbally abused and rolled your eyes at a rude male cashier. You've been traumatized and you deserve to be mad. This is the way you know how to protect yourself now, and I cannot judge you. I will not judge you anymore.

Instead, I'll hold close to us the one that we do love and trust. I'll remind of us the two men in our lives that we feel very fond and trustful of, something that feels both scary and exciting for us. I'll hold onto the idea that one day you will open, but I accept that for now you must be protective.

I love you,

skinned open

i did not ask to be the remains of a war zone:
these worn/torn bones of mine structure me into this form:
sharp cheekbones cut into their opinions of me

        & i am always better than what they think.

dark-skinned; heart pinned to my soul. i have
an odd nose, pearly drops of wisdom
teeth
& the smell of insomnia keeping me aloft.

they call me girl. i call me confusion.
they call me woman. i call me submissive.
      [ah! they say. don't you know woman & submissive are
synonyms for each other?]

they call me female. i call me alien.
sometimes i growl instead of whimper
& they laugh & call me a man
they think it's an insult.
i think it's a trap.

[because i've been told that men with sharp cheekbones
can cut more than just **opinions**]

they think calling me an anomaly is an achievement,

                      i think it is
                    f r e e d o m

but who cares what i think?
dark-skinned, submissive, worn/torn –

           i am an instruction manual for abuse
                a checklist for oppression
           a *how to get lost for dummies* book

[complete with audio cd]

but will you listen to me?

(untitled.)

the first time i told her i didn't like these lumps on my chest, she promised me she loved them. kissing, caressing, she breathed prayers into them and called me holy. i, she said, was her birth on venus, her statuesque goddess. i, once again, faced my own impossibility in the mirror of religion.

three months later, she held me down, this time with clenched fists instead of prayers reminding me how she loved the woman in me, the supple curvy waist and thighs, these doughy lumps on my chest. the pressure felt like nothing, a forced folding into myself.

she said i only disliked my lumps because of the misogynistic, racist queer culture that glorified white transmasculinity, testosterone, binders, and fundraisers for top surgeries.

the next week, she promised to love me back into acceptance with my body. she kissed and licked my breasts, buried curses or prayers deep into my breastplate. i can no longer distinguish holy utterances.

i learned a trick: pressure.

by applying pressure to myself, i molded my body into a shape i liked. i could reclaim the balled fists, the hands on my chest and body, the mouth that whispered into lumps of nothing. this daily act of pressure, now a ritual, is holy. i step into my binder, folding myself back into this body, resulting in sore ribs and weird posture. this chest – the recipient of 11 sir's, 3 ma'ams, 4 "i'm sorry's", and a lot of averted eyes on public transportation today – disrupts and soothes.

i don't let those sirs - hard fought for and never quite won – fool me; i don't escape misogyny or the violence of my past. my history – the night she knocked me down and flushed my anti-depressants down the drain in a dramatic sweep of apologies and refusals; the mornings she refused to let me leave her house; the control...now, my chest and i are who she never allowed us to be: self-determined.

two days ago, my friend sent me a poem. the poet stated, "there are ways of being a man that do not involve being a white man." there are ways of being masculine that do not involve racism, misogyny, violence, heavy/boisterous space-taking. the irony of masculinity being the refuge of violence and misogyny beats behind my breastplate, a strange phoenix refusing to be ignored wanting to destroy itself. i am reminded with each beat of a thousand old prayers spoken to my chest's strange existence and now blessed absence.

* * *

she had one thing right: the flesh stretched over my heart is holy. as i touch this skin today, i feel and hear beating, rhythmic life, controlled and articulated, organic and renewing.

i feel my chest rise slowly – barely tangible, each exhale a sigh of gratitude. my breath these days is short and shallow, no sudden gasps. i am no longer surprised when i feel that i cannot breathe; white masculinity greedily fights for space in my lungs, under my bones. not even my soul has a free pass from white supremacy.

chest, may we beat and breathe to a then-and-there one failure at a time, speaking and breathing holiness and forgiveness to all that you are. we are not yet whole.

A letter to my lungs

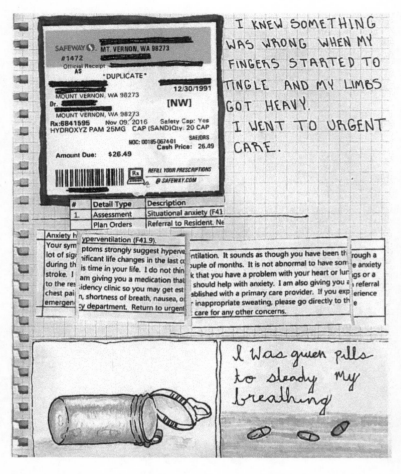

I knew something was wrong when my fingers started to tingle and my limbs go heavy. I went to urgent care.
I was given pills to steady my breathing.

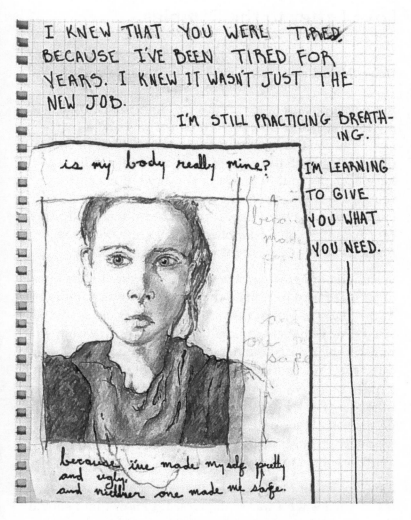

I knew that you were tired because I've been tired for years. I knew it wasn't just the new job. I'm still practicing breathing. I'm learning to give you what you need.
Is my body really mine? Because I've made myself pretty and ugly, and neither one made me safe.

Love Letter to the Dimples

Dear Dimples,

You have been the sole reason why I look pretty. Otherwise the long nose, the disfigured hips and one and a half lips, would not do anything to excite or titillate or for that matter oscillate through the pendulum of life. You have been my soul that bears the weight of my entirety, you have been my soul that gives away charms to all the cuties, you have been important and continue to be so, as I trespass through uninhibited charm, only thanks to your presence in the depressions of my cheeks.

Speaking of depression. I have been depressed quite often. At 7 I was raped by a male relative. At 12 I was gang raped. At the age of 7, I knew the taste of semen. Because of that, I had a very challenging childhood. I grew up with the impression of a disfigured body. I always thought I looked different, I thought my body was ugly. I took a bath some 7 times in a day just to ensure that I felt clean. Somewhere I thought that there were stains of blood or semen or urine on my body. It took me 11 years for the abuse to stop. It took another 5 for me to regain the steps of my life, and another couple to grow my wings.

I am sorry that I took so long to thank you for never leaving me when I was so depressed. I know that I should have acknowledged you, when the world took notice of you when I was too low to. I remember eavesdropping on a particularly bitchy conversation in college, where some girls were discussing what was "cool" in the college boys. One bitchy witchy woman said, "Well, there is nothing in you if not for your dimples." Well, I hated that the complete me was disregarded, because of the little patch of you in my face. All that mattered was you. Looking back, maybe, I should have reveled in joy for you were celebrated even when I as a whole was not. Maybe, I should have been happy for you are still an intrinsic part of me.

You have been a part of me. And you have always been a part of me. Even when I was a butt of jokes in college, when people busted me for being gay, you never left me. When people teased me, and bullied me, you never left me. You stayed with me in silent moments of joy that I felt while watching a movie. You were with me every time I felt a little happy and crazy. You never left me.

In fact, when I regained my life and I came out as gay, I had several compliments flowing my way. You were my most important feature. My dates would tell me, "I want to swim in your dimple" or "I love the depression, on your face," or the more messy, yucky, kinky, "Can I cum in your dimple"... It is funny, you can say, that I missed that you are my reason to be happy and sunny everyday.

You are my brethren, my family, my hope. You are my only dope. You are a part of me, yet you make the whole of me. I love you now and forever. And I hope when I am not so thrifty, in my fifty you don't leave me high and dry. With you, I can touch the limitless sky.

I know, for you, it is so very simple, but love, forever you are "my" dimple :)

I am thankful to you, that even I was depressed, and I paid no attention to the charm you brought to my face, I refused to see you.

I have received some dozen compliments.

You gave me a complex. And became the sole reason for me looking cute. You also were once my biggest flaw. I was cute, not macho. I was lovable, not feared.

To my Mind.

A while ago I set out on a journey that would forever change my life, and I was happy. Some might say I was stupid; probably out of my mind but it should be remembered that this mind of mine – was never my real mind in the sense it is for most people.

For as long as I can remember – who I am was always confusing, born at the start of World War Two I was a beautiful baby, still have the cute photos to prove it.

Looking deep into the eyes of my baby photos and into my mind would never show the real me. Neither would I know the real me for several years – in fact, it would take another 50 odd years to understand your view of who I was.

Everyone around me knew or so they thought, I was a baby Boy, I must have been because everyone said so and at my early age who was I to disagree – hell I couldn't even talk. These were the days when children were meant to be 'seen but never heard'.

For decades I lived a life others would see as normal, I did the usual boy things, then as time went by I married, had children, and buried myself in my work. Believing this was my normal, my life,– but at the same time realising something inside – you were telling me was not quite right – and there was nothing I could do about it.

The thoughts you insisted on never went away – confusing, terrifying – became almost the thoughts of a madman – and I knew if I was to survive they must be kept secret – hidden.

Actually life itself was not that bad, I always had a job and I was responsible, honest and dedicated, something I realise today was probably born about by the depth of the secret I held from the entire world.

As I became older this secret became so intense and my responses to it so demanding, its strength – you were simply impossible to ignore. So strong were the thoughts you gave me and their intensity – together with the knowledge that to release them would destroy me, made the possibility of taking my own life seem a very real way out.

Everything you told me seemed wrong but you never ceased – like a bad smell you never went away.

And there was another problem – I was weak and could never do that to my family it was something that was just not me – you had your own ideas of who I was.

Now in my early forties (a critical age) and with your confusion still strong as ever, I met a woman who changed my life.

A life with love became meaningful; something I realised the male in me had been missing. All that was new seemed to take away the things you told me, that had been bothering me for so long – get over it I reasoned a new path awaits.

In response to the real love of a wonderful woman I remarried, but here I also made the biggest mistake of my whole life and you never warned me, and that mistake – honesty – sharing my long-time secret with the love of my life, or in this case due to fear – deciding not to.

I ignored you and allowed that part of me you had always said was wrong – my maleness to take over.

Caught up in this new love I set aside all you had told me as the secret part of me magically dissolved into daily life, I had changed or so I thought. With my new married life, my work and the all-consuming challenge of building a home for the two of us. I actually believed love was all I ever only needed for the secret to go away – and for a time that seemed to be true – that what you actually told me might just be wrong.

And then it happened – an overseas bereavement in the family separated me from my love, even though it was only going to be a few months I was alone again, alone with only my thoughts and of course you.

Like a phoenix rising from the ashes – instantly I was back in my world of confusion, of secrecy – yet this time there was no choice – you were back stronger than ever.

There never was a back to normal again I was back into my old confused state once again. Still the weak and fearful person I always was, I continued my role you said was wrong – as the man. Never to mention my long held secret even to the only person in the world I respected, and loved.

Failing honesty at the very beginning of our relationship, I had unwittingly created for myself a lifetime of impossible guilt and you just let me get on with it.

For now a joyful even sexual marriage with love something so special that could never be put at risk, I had someone to live for, to love and be loved by – to tell her of my secret would surely destroy what we had together and I would be lost forever with death surely the only option.

So I continued my secret life, never realising the depth of compassion, of humanity my wife held for me. The day I finally told her my secret she was angry, desperate to understand how it was possible that this was happening to her.

We talked and she tried to understand the impossible – we walked in the park trying to get our heads around what we – she should do, she threw rocks at me in anger at the pain of what I had done to her, but the main problem – my big mistake – was that I was never honest with her in the beginning.

To this day I am still unsure which was the greater issue, the reality – or my dishonesty or not listening to you.

And the reality of my secret – I had to be the woman you had always said I should be. Except for the look of the body, which was definitely a man's, I was finally acknowledging to myself the reality of you and your unbelievable disclosure.

My thoughts ran rampant with impossible consequences, what had I done what could I do?

Death was too easy and, anyway, that complicated things even more – how could I do that to such a wonderful woman, this was not the way I did things.

But if ever there ever was a good time to take the easy way out – this was it. Thoughts of being alone, disgraced, banished from my children, my friends and almost certainly my job became my daily thoughts.

Thankfully the love I did not deserve, continued but never was quite the same, my secret stayed mine and now became my wife's.

Why she did not leave I cannot understand, but we stayed together, together, but somewhat distant. Thirty-odd years later we are still together with more of a friendship than a relationship, a kind of love and a life slightly different to what I believed would be normal.

I lost my job and retrained as a high-school teacher until it was my time to retire – meanwhile your secret evolved, continued the ongoing pain and everlasting guilt, I was slowly coming to accept what you knew all along: that I never was a man – but I still felt I was a desperate lie!

I even felt guilty at the way I presented myself to my students every school day, a fiction of a person I was not. Would they have understood if they knew, maybe some would, but for the most, like the rest of society, most likely they would not?

Now in my mid-sixties it was necessary to finally take control of my weakness, accept your view of my reality and become the real me. Tell the world – no more guilt but honour you – certain about all you had insisted – that '*I was a woman*'.

Somehow, whether it was that decision or the desire to set my life straight I am unsure, but a new path was clearly defined by all you had told me, many changes to be made, even a new name.

Later, at age 67, I travelled to Thailand for surgery to change my body, and my gender – forever. Having no longer any doubts about my decision I submitted myself to whatever was to follow, thoughts of major surgery at my age unimportant – if I could not be the real me I was past caring – I placed my destiny in you.

The gender reassignment surgery procedure went very well no pain, only sheer happiness in recovery, at the thoughts I was truly me at last. I do not think it possible for any cisgender person to understand the joy of knowing that your body – and you – my mind, were right and everything now, is as it should be.

Few will understand coming out of that kind of surgery at my age alone and in foreign country, to finally realise I had become the real me – truth is – words cannot convey the beauty and experience of such extreme joy.

All thanks to you my wonderful – persistent, and all-knowing – mind.

To my humble front entrance,

When talking about my transness, which most of us trans folks who get paid to string words together have to broach eventually, we have to consider you. You are, of course, one of the last things separating me from a garden-variety cisgendered male. Facial hair? I'm catching up in that department (thanks, testosterone.) An ample chest? Soon to be removed, thanks to the power of medical science. That leaves me with you, the little space between my legs.

I suppose it's not your fault you were stuck on me. If I'd asked for you, I suppose you were well enough. But you were hell in your own way.

Even when I tried in vain to embrace an identity more cohesive of your existence, you were a black hole. I'd reach a hand down between my legs and my fingers would reflexively clutch for a presence that wasn't there. You've stained many a pair of formerly favored boxers and briefs. When I would shower and forget to cover you with a towel when I stepped in front of the mirror, I'd marvel at your alien landscape, those peaks and craters that defined you.

Looking at myself, in general, tends to be a surreal experience, though less so as testosterone sculpts my face and body shape into something more recognizably me. But even as my jaw develops, no amount of T changes you. Hair almost makes you bearable, disguising the bumps and swatches of skin that lie beneath. The key word is almost.

One time, during my ill-attempt at womanhood, I squatted over a hand mirror and tried to map you out like this one feminist blog had implored me to do in order to connect with my inner feminine element, or whatever their euphemism for vagina was that day. I was supposed to come away from it with a newly cemented appreciation for my sexual essence. Instead, I nearly threw up. At the time I blamed it on being fat as if it made my pussy puffier or something.

In a weird little way, though, you existing at all helped me figure out that I wanted to transition, so I suppose you deserve some credit.

My ex loved you. Called bottom surgery "mutilation." He wasn't a smart man but he had some strong words for my body. I hated you for it. He fixated on you, demanded my body fit his mold for what was acceptable for a trans man to look like in his fantasies. An eventual hairy chest was okay but top surgery was right out. Forget about a meta or phalloplasty.

"You're lucky I'm even attracted to you," he'd tell me all the time. He was referring to you. "Gay men don't go for guys like you." I still, from time to time, wonder if that's true.

We've had some good times I suppose. We lost our virginity together. Sometimes, if I don't think about what you are, getting touched there feels pretty damn good.

Yet I still hate you. I have a nasty little secret that you know as well as I do. I freeze when shit happens. Knees lock and everything.

When it's never happened to you, you always think you'll be the one to knee the rapist in the crotch, push him to the floor, and run until you just can't. You're Rambo in your own head, you're better than just a victim. You don't say it but you turn your nose up at the people it happens to like they were too weak to know any better.

You remember when it happened. The first time it happened, he pinned me down against the bed. I couldn't fight. I wish you had. I wish you'd grown teeth, drawn blood. He didn't listen to my pleas. He called me a good girl because you existed. Because when he ripped off my boxers and my packer tumbled to the floor, he knew what I was and he didn't like it.

The second time someone did it, we still froze. You obliged him. All he had to do was force my legs apart. No matter how I pleaded, he didn't stop and you didn't bite back.

I'm back there every time I close my eyes. But I never really left.

A week after the first rape, I trudged into a community health clinic. I walked the two miles from my house as if all the predators in town would have smelled victim wafting from my pores if I'd taken the bus. "Just want to get checked out," I told the receptionist. "Just STD tests."

She slid a domestic abuse pamphlet into my hand.

I held up okay at first. Pissed in a cup and let them check if I'd gotten knocked up and swirled a Q-tip inside you by myself while a nurse stood outside the bathroom door. The exam was a different story. The nurse didn't even get a chance to probe me while I was splayed out on a paper-lined table with my pants off. I hyperventilated and slammed my thighs closed.

They sent me home with a paper bag full of condoms. I tossed them, along with the pamphlet, in my dresser drawer. I still have the pamphlet, though I never read it, floating around somewhere. I didn't do anything of the sort after the second rape. Maybe it was for the best.

My therapist tells me to stop blaming myself. I'm not trying to blame you. But I still get the impression that when I finally get my meta and they sew you up, a whole load of psychic weight's going along with you.

Goodbye. Sometimes I wish I could give you to someone who needs you more, but they'd have everything that happened to you go along with them. Maybe it's best if you just disappear like I used to pray you would as a child. I doubt it'll be the case but I hope you can take the nightmares with you.

an open letter to my body

(alternative title: me to me: all the
reasons why i trust in you)

voice: did i not give you enough space to grow? to flow
out & encompass words, hold them like i hold grief; rough
edges & a lisp: not feminine enough, a dirty cloth torn by
wolves. & i am a dirty cloth torn by wolves. they mocked
you, said you belonged to a man, but man is nothing but
the happening of hopes & breakages – yet i like to whisper
& fade into the night. i don't blame you for not wanting to
fade with me.

hands: smooth palms look pretty but shake when asked
to hold the knife. i want you to wield it. mother said she
could palm read once, & so we still wait patiently for the
people to turn their heads away. i ask you to write & you
scream. the trauma is hard, i know. so release it. let your
veins pop out, pave the crossroads to cross eyes. look into
them & make a fist & then ask yourself why some believe
you have the answers. still not thin enough, but nothing
else can pen the curl of the alphabet like you. alpha. beta.
(no, please don't beat her!) i put you to work, writing out
repression repeatedly & then complain when you fall apart.
i'm sorry that i hide under & fight with nothing that you
asked for. i will put you to better use, so learn! undress
me. disarm me. clench & unclench & release it all. believe
it more.

legs: carved out, hollow tree trunks with roots anchored
in no man's land. no man can walk with you, you're too
slow. i understand that walking is for those who have a
destination, but i am worthy of despair like all the others,

so let me run. i let you fall. is that not proof enough, that i am as fallible as the muscular junctions inside you? again, i let you fall, so return the favour tenfold & teach me freedom.

eyes: the window to my soul, blind – what does that say about the way i will navigate my heart? i know i am more machine than man; with compressed valves & an affinity towards breaking down. i, mechanical. i think i have seen too much of an emptiness so bleak that even rust daren't touch it – why bless something with fuel to live if it is to be condemned in darkness?

yet you have seen death & survived; how have i not thanked you before? i thank you now – i weep in gratitude & the tears mingle in the air. iron meets water & oxygen & you see the light.

& the rest: mania lives in the chest cavity where tachycardia never blessed so much as it did today, & will do tomorrow. i used to think of you as a cage but now i know you are the lock. there is always time to find a key, to find your place in the jigsaw, with a slight nose & gaping mouth – a wide gash across history.

my house, turned home – a cave filled with stories of the bloodline. a god-given tombstone carved out of the fears of all my ancestors. the master of all made me vessel of none: not girl, not boy – the theory undone.

* * *

i write to you with the deepest of sympathy. you have my condolences.

i am sorry i neglect you, but neglect is my mother tongue, so forgive me & forgive me again. forgive me & forget all i said.

yours ad infinitum,

the sharp pain of regret

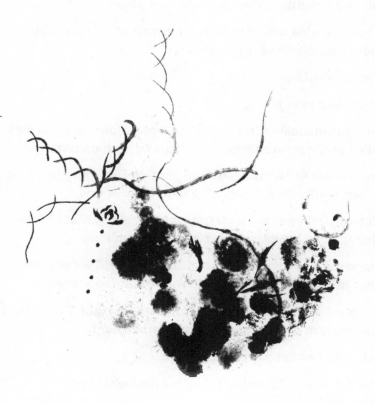

To My Grin,

You are beautiful below my nose and above my chin.

I have no idea where to start... I just want to thank you
from the bottom of my heart.

You've saved me.

Daily, you save me.

You continuously lift me up. Somehow allowing me to look
like I'm trying even when I'm seconds from giving up.

You ensure to everyone around me that I'm doing just fine.
When really, deep down, all I want to do is cry.

Convincing employers, despite my fumbling, that I'm the
one to hire. I swear, it's just my will crumbling.

Haggard and tired and worn from the world we're living
in. I just want to feel normal. Wanted and safe again.

It's hard when nothing seems to be going right. Every day I
feel like I'm gearing up to fight another fight.

But, see, I'm not worried anymore.

I'm not worried because I finally know what I'm
fighting for.

And I want everyone to know that even when I am fighting
I'm not alone.

Because you keep me open. My soul light; and happy
words spoken.

Ensuring to those around, despite my passionate anger, I
have my feet on the ground.

Firmly, I now stand tall with love in my heart. And you,
My Grin, you gave me that start.

I will treasure you every day and make you proud in every
way.

I may get nervous and feel a little queasy. I know that even
on the best days it won't always be easy.

But with you by my side, really, I no longer have to hide.

I thank you.

I love you.

Dear Vulva,

At five, I snapped a mirror in half with my heel, squatting awkwardly to see what was so interesting down there. You were probably already lost to conflicting discourse, uninvited pleasure dueling with staunch disgust; Mom's warning to leave you alone contradicting Rocco's praise that you were the cat's meow.

You were a lacuna for years. How did it feel to button your lip, to swallow your tongue? You tagged along like an annoying little sister on my dates. I muffled your cries by keeping on my pants, pushing lovers' hands and mouths away, cracking a joke. I read a lot about you to fill in the gaps, but you still rightfully belonged to someone else. You believed it was normal—the shroud, the drawn curtains, the dark hall.

Well, you learned how to be there and not there at the same time. A game to play, like hide and seek, where I stay in my head, and you don't want to be found. Did you grow impatient with my rainchecks for candles and incense? Did you vow to revolt if you weren't brought silk and prayers to the goddess? Did the words *dyke, woman, slut,* make you accept that your fate was to hover, to avoid?

It started as self-mocking to tell my new lover, oh, that's my front hole. He smiled, whispering, "I found something..." without needing to name you at all. He didn't call you tight or wet or hot. He didn't touch you like a test for how soon to get on top. He said you were an animal, an invertebrate. He trussed you up, pinched you til you squealed, smacked you like you were a bratty, spoiled imp, laughed at your long-in-the-teeth pout. He pet you for hours, called you a pelt, a cuteness, a little cock, an it. He refused to fill in the dotted line with pink, porn, and pussy. He revelled in your shape-shifting costume changes.

So can we make a fresh start? Hi. I'm not a girl or a boy. How are you? I'm fine, if a little lonely. Now, we're friends. There's lots of stuff to do together, hee hee, that we don't have to divulge. I guess my favorite part is sunny afternoons when I put on bad TV, lay out a towel, get good light, and pluck your hair into special shapes. It gives me a chance to look at you up close, to learn your amethyst wrinkles and fritillary edges. Does it feel like getting dressed up? Like, ah, I'm ready to be teased and admired, pinched and spoiled, to make your debut as the sassy star, and come out for the curtain call and bow, and dozens of lilies thrown from front row, and the smell of perfume fills the theater, pearlescent and heady.

A Song for My Voice

I. "BABYSOFT."

The other night, when you sang "For Today I Am a Boy" in class, I uncovered a new side of you.

I had misgivings about singing that song: Anohni wrote it about being a transfemme, and I am not of that experience. But she also wrote that song, I think, about being a nonbinary femme, and that is what I (currently) am. I have listened to that song on repeat to unlock facets of my own gender. I too have felt like a permanent child until I started to step into my "true" gender, if such a thing exists. It feels like a second puberty.

I've been on a journey with Anohni for a while now too. When I was 19, and closeted, my butch boss clocked me by saying that Antony and the Johnsons was my soul band, and that I should really listen to them. I subsequently avoided that band for a long time because I knew, on some level, what it would mean for me to hear the music.

I recalled this as I took the stage and looked out at my audience of peers, running a mental reel of stories around how my choice of song might affect each person in the room. Act-OUT is an acting class for people of LGBT experience, founded by Brad Calcaterra in response to a slew of suicides by queer youth in the US. The class, in many ways, is an exercise in shame resilience. We take the things that make us want to self-destruct and turn them into art. It's also a community-building exercise. We talk often in class about the ways in which our community is united and divided. I remember looking at my transwomen friends in the front row and wondering if I had their permission to sing this song. Brad gives us a lot of permission in that room, but it doesn't always align with the permission we give ourselves or each other.

The physical setting intensified the stakes of my choice too. The cavernous theater at the LGBT Center in Manhattan is a converted basketball court, where Act-UP had meetings and AIDS victims were cared for during the crisis. Countless meetings, rallies, speeches, clinics, dance parties, and functions have filled that enormous space. The energy of our forebears permeates the room. The mise-en-scène adds to the grandeur. A giant purple velvet curtain adorns the back wall, drawn together ceremoniously by two students at the beginning of every class, usually to a soundtrack of Sylvester, Donna Summer, or Madonna. A portable spotlight bathes a center aisle, where every student does a catwalk and solo dance at the beginning of class. Rows of chairs with students waiting to work flank the aisle. Though the vibe is congenial and supportive, when students work the audience attention is laser-focused: Nobody eats, talks, texts, or looks away.

As I sang the opening lines I energetically shrank. The teacher, Brad Calcaterra, caught me. He could see the shame kickback unfurling. Brad asked why I was looking down. I told him that I was trying to look at the audience. He told me to let the audience come to me. I received that, and stood up straighter, relaxing, letting the sound fill the room.

Initially I had tried to sing "powerfully," emitting a big sound like Anohni does at the end of the song. I had this idea that power = loud, strong, *forte*, because that had been true of how I have learned to wield you, my large, deep Voice. Brad countermanded, telling me to soften, quieter, quieter...*quieter*. "Babysoft," he said. I resisted. As my voice crept up in volume he brought me back down again. By the time I was singing the last line, "For today I am a child/For today I am a boy," the song had become a lullaby. A lullaby for *every* confused and sad thought that any child has *ever* had about their gender at any fucking point.

I had been staring at the exit sign as I delivered my performance. Once I finished I circled my gaze back to people in the room, and saw that my friends were crying.

II. "BANSHEE."

To have a deep voice and to be assigned female at birth is to be monstrous.

It happened in the first grade, first.

One of the 25 girls in my first-grade class at Perth College, An Anglican School for Girls, made fun of me because I couldn't scream as high as the other girls when we were playing chasey. I noticed it myself before she said anything. I couldn't have screamed as high as the other girls if I tried. *And I did try.*

In the seventh grade, four or five of us were sitting at adjacent desks, whispering back and forth under our breath while the teacher was speaking. It was innocent enough: The teacher had more or less called for quiet at the beginning of class, so we hushed as we squeezed out the last of our lunchtime chatter.

I was the only one who got in trouble.

The teacher leveled with me in front of the class: "Listen, I know you weren't the only one speaking—you just have a low voice, and low voices carry, so you're more likely to get caught. Something to bear in mind as you get older."

In the ninth grade, my choral teacher discovered my ability to sing a high tenor. I still had the lowest voice in my class, and was already an Alto II. The other girls whispered to each other under their breath as I hit the low notes. I had been bullied *every day* since the first grade so this was standard fare. It still enraged me.

In the tenth grade, my voice teacher thought that
I was pressuring my voice down. "Sometimes girls will
do that, to seem like they have more authority," she said.
After running a few scales with me she realized, a little
bashfully, that she was wrong.

That same year I decided to emancipate you, Voice.
I wanted to take up a martial art outside of school.
My anger needed an outlet, I wasn't great at team sports,
I had been bullied for nine years at the Perth College,
and I really needed to be around some boys. I had barely
been around boys at all growing up, and it deeply messed
with my self-esteem, my gender identity, and my sense
of comfort. The scant few times that I had been around
boys had always been staggeringly simpler and more
comforting than the endless maze of all-girl popularity
politics that ravaged my school days. I wanted more.

I ended up joining a local fencing gym at the
university near my house. Having a space to socially self-
express outside of the uniformed former convent that was
my high school activated every latent impulse in me. I got
a boyfriend, tried out polyamory, had several trysts with
and crushes on teen girls, cut off all my hair and dyed it
cherry red, tried booze and pot, and started fencing sabre,
first interstate and then internationally. I howled and
screamed at my opponents, part-tactic and part-catharsis,
earning me the nickname "The Banshee," as if my sounds
hailed Death itself.

I first unlocked you, Dear Voice, through fighting, at
home, at school, and on the fencing strip. For a while that
was the only way I knew how to unleash your power.

Time passed, and things grew darker. My boyfriend
violated my boundaries, crushing my sexuality, and
scaring me away from polyamory for many years. My
female teen lover spiraled out into drugs and alcohol,
later confessing to me that her dad had been sexually

abusing her. I moved back into the closet and away from home. I took an almost scholarly interest in every drug I could find. I quit fencing.

Then I got accepted into Yale, and would be joining the varsity fencing team in the fall. With the help of my confused, beleaguered parents, I sorted out my financial aid, quit drugs, went to a homeopathist to rebuild my central nervous system, took up fencing again, got my paperwork in order, and permanently left Australia.

Time marched on, but the othering on vocal grounds remained constant. As a brand new freshman at Yale, a world away from my hometown, a new friend in my residential college told me that they found me "intimidating" because of my "deep voice."

About a year and a half ago, a friend of mine told me that I have a "man in my voice." I said "Thank you."

About ten months ago, I was playing a round of Hot Seat with some friends and my new lover, now my partner, whom I had recently met on Tinder and was in the process of socially vetting. In this game, somebody receives questions from the audience, selected by a moderator, and responds by either telling the truth, lying, or saying nothing. A friend of mine asked my partner what had been most surprising about me when we had met for the first time, after two months of digital correspondence. He replied, "Her voice."

How many times have we been called "scary," "loud," "aggressive," "intense," "powerful," "full-on," just because you, my Voice, are deep?

What are the things that make you so low? Is it hormones? Genetics? Fate? Past lives? Growing up in a dry climate? Pollution? Screaming as a kid?

A man trying to escape the cage of his own body?

III. "SIR?"

If a cashier hears me before seeing me, they will say, "Sir."

If I wear my Carhartt in the winter with my hood up and a stranger bumps into me, he will say, "Sorry, sir."

When I was sixteen and had short hair, I was reading a book on an airplane, hunched over my tray table. A flight attendant hovered over me: "Sir..."—I looked up—"... Madam!"

I don't know if it's you, Voice, or if it's my above-average height for my assigned gender, or if it's my perpetual-beginnings of facial hair, but I can literally have my waist-length hair down and lipstick on and somebody will "sir" me.

Strangers can read my hybrid energy and they don't even know it.

IV. "DEEP."

One of the privileges of having a deep voice is that people assign authority to me when I wield it. In this civilization, where masculinized voices are deemed worthy of the *polis*, and anything else is relegated to the hysterical or beastly, my voice is a hidden superpower. If I raise you, Voice, to command a room, everybody immediately goes quiet. People constantly tell me to host a radio show, and for a while I did. When I lead guided meditations people relax very quickly.

Do people find the voice of authority soothing? Or am *I* just soothing?

Recently, I asked my partner about our first encounter again, and what he thought about my voice when he met me. I wanted more information: I assumed that my voice had impacted him in a negative way, and I was still vaguely hurt about it.

My partner said that my voice had pleasantly surprised him. It resonated inside his body in a way that made him feel warm and safe. He said it felt like a good sign, and that it felt "deep."

"Deep like what—like my voice was deep, or the connection was deep, or the effect on you was deep?"

"In all senses of the word."

V. "STOP."

My "voice of authority" doesn't always work.

One night on Christmas Eve, five years ago, my mum, best friend and I all went to a bar to get drunk. We met a set of 26-year-old Colombian twins and their little brother. I took one of the twins home. We fucked. It was rough. Partway through I decided that I had had enough. So, Voice, we said "Stop."

We had to say "stop" six times before he pulled out, reluctantly and with much resentment.

Do you remember all the times when people silenced you or made you wrong?

When my ex, who got me pregnant, gave me herpes, and cheated on me, would shout us down, or hang up on us every time we spoke our truth?

When our freshman rugby player friend forced us into oral sex after we said "No no no no no"?

When we would speak up about my assault as a teenager and "friends" would laugh at us?

When you tentatively revealed that you were gender-questioning to two of your parents, and one of them said "I disagree; I think you're very much a woman"?

IV. "WEEPING."

I am a performance artist, and one of my characters is a Primal Scream Therapist. I have processed a lot that way: Onstage, in front of a packed house, guiding everybody into an ear-splitting Primal Scream. It was so easy for me to loose my voice in this way after my years on the fencing strip. Roaring, bansheelike, I brought the house to its knees. *This, I would think, is POWER.*

It wasn't until this past summer, at Sufi Camp of all places, that I met an actual Primal Scream Therapist. "Primal has a very bad reputation for being a rage-type therapy," she told me. "Only about 5% of it is rage. The rest is very deep weeping."

* * *

Voice, we have done a lot of things over the past year. Screamed at the top of our lungs; shrieked like Janis Joplin and Tina Turner; pulled off hyperbolic Australian accents as we contorted into characters that made our comrades howl with laughter. Raced up the energetic ladder to top a scene partner in acting class. Chanted for hours at a time. Sang queer love songs at radical faerie sanctuaries. Taught Neapolitan spell-songs to dispel depression. Found myriad ways to tell the truth of what has happened to us.

It has been great to give you a space to express everything locked inside. Over the months we have relearned that aggression comes easy to us, as does volume. Our power in the *forte* is undisputable.

The deepest healing power all year, though, might have emerged from singing a babysoft lullaby to a crowded room.

What new power is this?

To my hair,

I'm sorry I spent so many years hiding under you. I thought of you as a weighted curtain that could conceal me as my body started to change. You and my loose clothes were curated by careful neglect: no-one could accuse me of trying to look like a pretty girl if it was obvious I left you trailing split ends and ragged threads on purpose. No-one would touch me again if they couldn't see the skin underneath you. For years, I pretended to be merely an unkempt girl rather than an unsolvable problem.

My mother remembers adoring you: when she thinks of us, she thinks of a wave of loose brown curls, the body underneath in a joyful hurry. She remembers me being such a happy child and I remember being so angry – angry at what I couldn't exactly remember had happened to our body that night, angry at everything – I would pull you out in bunches and cry for the lost depth of your coverage.

I never learned how to adorn you. I remember preening when my father braided you and then panicking because when you were pulled back, my face could not hide. I left you loose and growing, parting you in the middle so you would hang over both sides of my face. I avoided getting you cut so I wouldn't have to look in the mirror at the salon. When I did go, at my mother's urging, I would see my face twitch as I stuttered or see the gaps between my teeth. I needed you all the more at these places where the men's side of the building was detailed with stained pine and chrome, the women's side had painted roses in profusion, and the entrances were separate. I was a fraud on either side and I still needed you to hide me.

I cut you and kept you short for years after the rape that I remember. I had you shaved because you had not hidden me, and it was a distraction to marvel in the absence of your weight rather than remember the other weights on top of me, whether vaguely on my back or in wretched detail on my belly.

Recently, we have become reacquainted. You are a stranger on my shoulder but I want to get to know you. I remake that binary-pinched building now that I am trying to learn how to gently shape you. I look up online tutorials, buy hairpins and get frustrated when the lessons assume I know the basics of working with you. Ruefully, I look up "how to make a man bun" in the hopes that those guides might assume less about my skill-base.

Touching you is both an act of forgiveness and apology. My father is going to teach me to braid you.

to my back,

the chiropractor didn't touch you
instead she said to the rest of us
what you used to protect yourself
years ago
is now only hurting you
if you keep making yourself small
your back is only going to get worse
i wish i knew
how to stop
making you small
i am sorry
i never stretch you towards
the sky
i am sorry
i care more about hiding my breasts
than your wellbeing
i am sorry
every possible solution for your pain
seems temporary
i am sorry
everything that still hurts
keeps climbing up your ladder
i hope it never makes it back to
the top
where my brain decides it's better
to let the ladder
fall
i am sorry
you hurt the most after having sex
even when the rest of us feels
soft and present

you cannot move
you trick yourself
into thinking survival means
laying flat
do you know
how hard we have worked
to be soft and present
do you know
how many people die every year
from fallen ladders
i never told my high school
friends
why you flinch
so much
i am sorry
i did not stand up for you
their laughter made you curve
down
little by little
when you misinterpreted
a hug
a passing of the popcorn
a gift
as a state of emergency
do you know love
you are no fire escape
do you know love
when indigo said
you can stay
here
she really meant it
don't bend over backwards
to leave
like it or not

there is someone
watching out for you
from up top
shouting down
release
everything
except
your own
life.

Dear Brain,

I used to feel as though you were a scary and unpredictable person. I lived with the fear of what you would do next. What you'd make me do, feel, think. Like an angry infection, you've been burning for years, enraged and always active. Between the infection and the mental illness, you always seemed to have a life of your own. And that scares me.

You have ways of stopping me dead in my tracks, extinguishing the sunshine in a matter of moments and leaving me lost in the dark. You've put a knife in my hand, voices in my head, and a bottle to my lips to keep the demons at bay. You make me forget, cause me to stumble over my words, and sometimes even paralyze my whole body.

But since starting meds, a venture you took to well, I realized you weren't out to hurt me at all. That all these years you were screaming for help, you were hurting. And I angrily silenced you instead of listening to the eloquence of your words, expressed in classic bipolar symptoms that you've been communicating since my childhood.

But with what felt like the whole world against us, it was easy to slip into hating you. My family hated what you did to me, and yelled at me excessively for it. As if your actions were under my control. If yelling, bullying and hitting cured the voices and the pain, you would've been quieted long ago. Instead, you only got angrier and louder.

So I started to listen.

I slowly learned your language, as I deciphered your messages. We identified concrete symptoms that were plaguing you, going from blurry and mysterious suffering to "depression," "anxiety" and "mania." With your help and patience, I slowly learned who you are. We learned "bipolar" was a safe and comfortable label to tack onto you in order to get you proper treatment. And now that I take better care of you, taking pills that you seem to quite like, at least three times a day, the messages have changed.

You communicate when there's not enough mood stabilizer or too much antidepressant.

You tell me that you're happy, and I hesitate in believing you. We've both got a lot of adjusting to do, living this new life with a newly balanced you. But in the meantime, we revel in the happy magic of feeling sane for the first time in our lives. Even if that feeling is sometimes fleeting.

At this point, I feel as though I know you better than anyone in my whole life. I'm sorry for not listening to you when I was younger, for silencing you and prolonging your suffering. No matter how much I've been told to, I will never hate you. You challenge me, which is hard on the both of us. But I love you unconditionally, and will fight for the rest of my life for you. Never again will I turn away when you cry out to me for help. You are safe, I am safe, we are safe with each other.

Love,

Dear Body:

You have been, through your time on Earth, a veritable site of Foucauldian trauma. We took the clinical gaze into our bones when we survived Cipro before the FDA updated its Black Box warning on neurotoxicity. We learned to walk on broken tendons and nerves as life became a Proustian blur tinged with DuChampian overtones. It's a period we still refer to as "À la recherche du temps perdu en la fontaine"—for we were stuttering as we learned to speak and write again—tracing the paths of Moraga, Albee and Butler through Malinche, Zoo Stories, and gender performance.

Our brain first changed in utero, when Mother signed a waiver and took the estrogen injection to keep us safe and warm for two more months. She was scared of losing, since she lost already, but she proclaimed us as broken and stunted from that moment forward. It wasn't the cigarettes she smoked as she grieved the loss of her brother who died in a car filled with carbon monoxide with his friends while making a drug run. It wasn't the grief our family felt when Grandfather lost the light rail mill in negotiations between the Local 65 and U.S. Steel top brass, with Reagan using his face and plight as the example of the high price to pay for unionization.

We were upset when Grandmother told us we couldn't grow up to be a boy when we were five, even though we learned the physical reasons why from a picture book with flowers and mommies and daddies who loved each other very much with penises and vaginas when we were three. We almost went deaf from ear drum ruptures related to black mold and indoor smoking. We vaguely remember a

pink towel, a sugar cookie, and an uncle who took what
didn't belong to him in Colorado, because the memory
suddenly came back to us when we had sex for the first
time sober with a husband who would rape us many, many
times—and have a Chaplain Major come to have us cuffed
and thrown in the back of a police car—and shot up with
Risperdal in rural Louisiana when we were bold enough to
ask for a divorce.

We remember the time he actively translated Leviticus
to prove that what he was doing was not rape because
you were female, and he was male, and married—and
we have trusted nothing about God or government since.
We remember the time we almost ran over our mother's
foot one Christmas because she tried to convince us our
father was involved. He got mixed up in a lot of things.
He ran weapons in Kane County during the Cook County
registration moratorium. But we already know he never
touched you with less than love and respect.

We got our freedom eventually, when our two trans friends
came to burst us out of hell. We were felled by
pharmaceuticals, time and rage. We still struggle to stand.

Body, we both know who
owns you, no matter what
they told Carrie Buck or
Henrietta Lacks.

Body, we claim you
every single day, as we
flow through gender
uninterrupted, peeing in
neutral bathrooms and

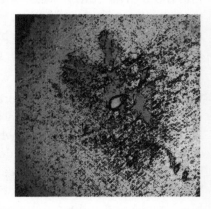

cumming and screaming your acceptance with every
shudder and quake.

Hello,

This is a short note from the author of the following two letters:

These essays contain mentions and descriptions of sexual assault, mentions of child sexuality, a description of a session with a Sacred Intimate (SI), and explicit descriptions of sexual contact, desire, and fantasy. Some of the sexual content transpired when I was a teenager, younger than the legal age of consent in some US states.

Writing these essays was a liberating experience for me, and an essential aspect of my own healing. Naming my desires, new and old, and revealing these scenes from my life—writing all of it down, no matter how battered, bruised, or broken, no matter how questionable when laid against my current politics and identities—that changed me. I feel able to say "These things happened to me; my experience as a whole and complex person is completely valid" in a way that I never felt able to before.

Taking that declaration further, I chose to publish these essays online as you find them here, with an author by-line and a content warning. They have been well received by survivors and nonsurvivors, trans, nonbinary, cis, queer and straight people alike. With that said, though, please do what you need to take care of yourself if you choose to read on, and if you want to end your experience of the book here, that is beautiful too. I would never, ever want my words of self-liberation to re-imprint trauma in another.

Additionally, the publishers would like to advise caution when seeking out a Sacred Intimate to work with, and I agree. Any intimate exchange should be entered into with a clear understanding of boundaries and consent, as well as a sense of your compatibility with the practitioner on a healing and safety level.

Here are some helpful questions to ask yourself or your partners or if you choose to find a Sacred Intimate in your area:

- *Has a member of your community, or somebody you trust, vouched for them as a practitioner?*

- *Do they put you at ease?*

- *Will they respect your body, and your pronouns?*

- *Will they use the correct terminology for your body parts?*

- *Do they know what your triggers and boundaries are?*

- *Have you shared you "nos" with them?*

- *Have they asked for your safe words?*

- *Do you feel ready for a session or do you still need more time?*

Having sensual and sexual contact with a relative stranger for the purposes of healing is very intense. I chose to have that experience when I was ready. There were many years before that where I barely had any sexual contact in any capacity.

Take care of yourself,

A Wide-Open Letter to My Mouths

[This letter contains explicit and sensitive material – please read the author's note on pages 128–129.]

Dear Mouths,

Recently, a new lover retaught me how to eat a mango.

We were naked on a rock, in a stream, somewhere in Virginia, long hair wet against our bodies: Two shimmering mountain mermaids. On the second day of our solar eclipse pilgrimage to Short Mountain, Tennessee, in a polycule of lovers, we had managed to steal away to find a pocket of time, a creek, and a mango to share together. I was excited and nervous, giggling and bantering wantonly as I pulled her close to me on the rock. Water, catching the rays of the sun, glinted as it swirled around us, beading on our sweating bodies.

Intertwining my legs with hers, I sat up straight to meet my lover's gaze, grinning broadly, pucklike, as I took the mango from her hands and wedged it between us. My lover initially smiled and giggled back at me; then the smile tensed into something else as a flush crept up her cheeks. She receded from my gaze. I felt her tense slightly where our bodies touched. I asked what was going on for her. My blushing lover took a deep breath, and opened her heart to me.

There had been prior shared mangos. Some of those times were beautiful, others disappointing or chaotic. Fruit-sharing with lovers who weren't fully present or appreciative really let her down. To guard against this scenario with the large, viscous, and sticky mango, my lover first vetted people with lower-impact fruit. She had already shared a peach, two plums, and some cherries with me before our mango, so she *knew*, she said, that I "got it."

In that moment, though, recent life events had left her feeling vulnerable. Sharing that particular mango with me, then, would be a sacred and historic act for her. A healing ritual. I understood, then, that my lover was still vetting me: Reminding me that she was initiating me into *her* practice. I nodded; receiving and affirming as best I could as she exhaled. I *did* get it. In our shared nectary, fruit is a vessel, a kink, and a prayer.

I didn't say it, but I was nervous too. Nervous and excited to meet a person who spoke the same sex language as me. More than once I had watched her mind flood with images of what might transpire in our shared reality. This *titillated* me.

While she was talking, my lover massaged the mango until it seeped translucent yellow nectar from its nipple. I felt my own nipples coming to life as I watched her work.

When the time came, she brought the mango to my lips.

"Remember, no teeth," she reminded me. I had rushed earlier fruit foreplay by tearing chunks from the flesh. I smiled at her coyly, and nodded. Then I put you, sweet Mouth, Upper Mouth, on the mango's nipple and sucked, long and hard.

I kissed my lover, and passed some of the nectar into her upper mouth. She used her tongue to gently and precisely stroke the tip of mine in a way that made me moan and pant; mouths wet, clit tingling. I imagined her tonguing my clit when she kissed me like that. We discovered that I could stimulate myself if I massage the tip of my tongue with my finger: my clit would tingle and I would get wet. My two mouths love to communicate.

Soon enough, my upper mouth and the mango were all over her. Nectar was everywhere.

Mouths—would that I could give you this sort of healing all the time. We've whispered, screamed, ejaculated, menstruated, eaten, overeaten, shared secrets, spoken harshly, queefed, pleasured, gasped, contracted, broken out, scolded, drooled, oozed, scissored, discharged, miscarried, forgiven, prayed, bitten, sucked, ovulated, made love. You are my nourishment portals—I can't live without you. I love the shapes you make when you are getting what you want, when you are thinking, smiling, frowning, contracted, relaxed, clenched, pursed, engorged, wet, salivating. I have covered you in lipstick, fruit, ejaculate, lube, and other bodies. I have bled out of you. I have waxed your hair and let it grow. I have brushed my teeth and neglected hygiene. I have changed my diet to fix you. I have fixated on you. I use you to pleasure and protect each other, and me.

This is my love letter to you, Mouths.

* * *

In my freshman year at Yale, a fellow freshman forced me to suck his dick while I was drunk. He was strong; he played rugby. He was wasted. He was also my friend.

I was drunkenly walking this friend home after a party. We cuddled in his bed. Then we made out. Suddenly, my friend pulled down his pants to expose his erect cock and forced my mouth onto it. You said "No no no no...no..." didn't you, Upper Mouth? "No no no" until you and I gave up and sucked his dick.

The next day, we met up to talk, and he apologized.

"I am so...so...sorry," he said, his voice quavering. We were exiting the local deli, Gourmet Heaven. We had just

gotten sandwiches. I had ordered a hero with smoked
turkey, brie, and green apples, with honey mustard.

I looked at him. "I forgive you," I said. I thought I
meant it too. I even gave him a hug, ostensibly because I
wanted to, though I've since wondered if I was acting on
a lifetime of programming to compulsively care for men
ahead of my own wellbeing. *I forgive you for assaulting
me; here's a hug to soften the blow of your crushing burden of
remorse.*

We parted ways, sandwiches in hand. I didn't really
see him or interact with him much ever again.

The next day, it all hit me. I dissociated; couldn't think,
could barely focus on work or class; I felt numb, confused.
Angry. I started meekly asking around about how to notify
Yale College of a sexual assault on their campus. I wasn't
even sure if there was a difference between a charge and
a complaint; I just wanted them to know, and I wanted
something to be done.

The process was oblique, to say the least.

Once I had found the correct avenue, through some
asking, I found myself sitting on a couch opposite a grim,
unsympathetic-looking woman with an air of resigned
bureaucracy. Her attire was plain, bordering on drab;
her grey hair pulled back into a taught bun. The room
was dark.

My interviewer perched on the edge of a chair
opposite me, and asked me what had happened. I
recounted the events as I recalled them and she listened,
impassively.

I finished, and all was quiet. Then:

"Did he rape you?"

"Um...no...?" *Are my mouths so different?* "He forced me
to into oral sex."

"Was he sorry?"

"*What?*"

"Did he tell you he was sorry?"

"...yes?"

"Then there's nothing we can do."

I pushed her on this. I wanted to press charges. I wanted something, *anything*, to happen. She didn't budge.

A few months later, I was in Amsterdam with a lover ten years my senior. We had met at the 2007 Asian Fencing Championships in Nantong, China, both competing for Australia in different weapons, and hailing from different states. I lay on my stomach, face down on a sprawling, plush bed on the top floor of an open-plan townhouse, and made him fuck me from behind, thrusting his dick into me until I wailed with pleasure. We came, and then I asked him to hold me while my body convulsed, wracked with sobs. I told him about the assault then. He consoled me, sweetly but cluelessly. Almost vacantly. I could tell that he didn't really know what to do. Receiving that vacant comfort was almost worse for me than keeping the news inside. How far away men can sometimes be from the violence of other men.

I was with my mother and sister on that trip, and I ended up telling my mother about the assault the next day. She brushed it aside quickly, too troubling for her to look at. Six months later she apologized, and it was my turn to brush it aside. In that initial moment, though, the weight of pervasive, collective dismissal from lover, institution, and mother crushed both of my mouths shut. I sat on my secret and my sex life dried up.

My assailant went on to reoffend, unreprimanded, multiple times, and graduate with an Ivy League degree.

The same year that he and I both graduated, some very brave Yale feminists did two things: revive *Broad Recognition*, a feminist magazine that I wrote many articles for, and file a Title IX complaint against Yale University that was upheld, forcing the school to redo their entire system for processing sexual assault claims. The Title IX complaint had 22 cases in it: 22 among thousands. I wanted to add mine, Mouths, but I realized that three celibate years later I still felt too broken from the experience to let either of you speak the truth for me.

* * *

Mouths, you have always healed each other. Learning how to have great sex has given me a rich and resonant voice, and license to tell the world about what has happened to me. Learning how to vocalize my pain and pleasure had led me to energetically dearmor my genitals. Examples of this are numerous, Mouths, but I want to recall a very direct and recent story about both of you, and how you interacted to make me feel better.

I sessioned with a Sacred Intimate (SI) recently: A warm and handsome middle-aged queer man who had played with me at a kink retreat a month or two before. It was the dead of winter then. I had melted in his hands as the snow piled up outside.

The job of a Sacred Intimate, I would say, is to cocreate a sensual/sexual container with a client in order to witness and facilitate a self-healing process. After the kink retreat I decided to become an SI someday, since sexual healing is already a part of my life. I gave my friend a call, ostensibly to ask him about his profession. I ended up arranging to travel upstate for a session. I told myself that it was a "research trip." My body, meanwhile, geared up for an emotional and physical release: I became anxious as the day approached.

As my SI drove me to his house from the bus station, he noticed that I was tense, and asked me how I was feeling. I told him that I was nervous. I wondered if he would find this surprising. The last time we had seen each other he had undressed me, handcuffed me, and strung me up by the padded cuffs with a length of rope stretched over a beam in the middle of a sex party, flogging me front and back until I shrieked with pleasure. We were not exactly strangers to each other's bodies, and I wasn't nervous about being with him sexually again. It was for other reasons: I had never paid for sex before, nor had I ever really had complete transactional license to ask for exactly what I want in bed.

"Have you thought about what you want to do in the session?" he asked gently, as we approached our destination. I shook my head and cast my eyes downward. Approaching this frontier of sexual healing had left me bereft of my connection with my desire.

We arrived. I showered and changed. We sat on his porch and looked at the forest, grey and beautiful, still devoid of leaves in the early spring. It was warm that day. I felt ungrounded, jittery with nerves and the energy of the city, so I asked for help to become present. My SI nodded, and gestured that we go inside. He stepped behind me, and gently but firmly grabbed me by the scruff of my neck. I immediately became aroused.

Applying firm and even downward pressure to the back of my neck and shoulders, my SI took me on a tour of his workrooms. There was what appeared to be a stimulation room, with a St. Andrew's Cross and all manner of floggers and toys, and a destimulation room, filled with mats, cushions, and essential oils. My SI picked up one of the essential oils and held it under my nose, asking me to breathe it in. Walnut oil. I immediately felt my energy come back into my body and surge down my legs into the earth.

We traveled to the other room, sat in a cushioned nook near the cross, negotiated our boundaries, and checked the time. My two hours began.

My SI undressed me, blindfolded me, and cuffed me.
In the first half of the session he cuffed me to and flogged
me against the cross, talking dirty to me, sucking my
nipples and teasing my clitoris until I begged him to finger
me. I strained against my cuffs.

I dissociated once. I went to a place of anxiety and
doubt: I was in a stranger's house, in an undisclosed
location, where nobody could hear me scream. I had spent
a lot of money on this experience. I was tracking my ever-
present attraction to Daddy Doms, wondering how that fits
within my politics. My mind went anywhere but that room.

My SI quickly noticed and brought me back. Whatever
fluctuations happened in my body were duly registered
and responded to in a safe, sane and consensual way. In
my sexual history and experience, this level of attention
and sensitivity is very special and rare.

Once my SI was fingering my lower mouth, and I
started to approach climax, he would have me tell him
when I was about to cum and then he would pull his
fingers out, allowing me to crest by myself, riding on the
wave of my own pleasure. Soon enough I was gushing
down my legs and onto the cross.

My voice started to open: This experience of climactic
solitude was unimaginably powerful. "Be as loud as you
want," my SI whispered to me. My volume wavered with
my sense of safety. Whenever my voice closed, my SI would
coax it open again, lovingly affirming my right to vocal
expression, no matter how loud or monstrous.

I have always been loud during sex. My voice is
low and resonant, and carries far. *Upstairs* neighbors
have yelled at me to "SHUT UP!" as I fucked. During that
session, however, the sounds I made were some other thing
entirely—louder and more monstrous than ever before. I
filled the woods with my sound. I blew open all the doors

and shook every tree. My silken, beastly grunts shattered
walls within me.

One mouth heals the other.

My SI knew when I needed a break. He led me, still
naked, cuffed and blindfolded, to the destimulation
room, which was smaller and ringed with a waist-high
ledge brimming with essential oils. Mats and cushions
covered the floor. My SI lay me down, propped up my
head with a pillow, uncuffed me, and enveloped me with
his body, pulling a blanket over us and asking me if I was
comfortable, if I needed anything.

He then asked me to describe to him what was going
on with each of my chakras, from the quality of brightness,
to the color, to anything else I could see. I energetically
scanned my body and relayed what I saw. My lower three
chakras were bright and vibrant; my fourth chakra, over
my heart, was wavering, static-y, trembling. My upper
three chakras, in particular my throat chakra, were dim.

My SI explained this back to me in terms that I
could understand. Orgasmic energy generated in the
lower pasture needed to be sent *across the dam that was my
diaphragm* to nourish and feed the upper pasture. This
could be achieved by breathing in sharply every time I had
an orgasm. For one mouth to feed the other, there needed
to be a bridge.

We decided that my SI would continue to hold me,
still blindfolded, in the destimulation room, and massage
my lower mouth. He called it a "yoni massage," but as a
nonbinary human I prefer gender-neutral terms for my
genitals.

I rode the waves of pleasure in my dark den
and breathed in every time a wave crested, moaning
ecstatically. It continued this way for a while, and then
all at once my in-breath turned into little gasps, which
turned into sobs, and I felt so young; too young. My mind

became populated with images of my first boyfriend, starting with the uncomfortable and rushed way that we had lost our virginity to each other, and blossoming into all of the ensuing cruelty and abuse in our relationship. I was screaming and crying and cumming and mourning that it *wasn't supposed to happen that way*, as a tidal wave of repressed violence around my sexual awakening broke over me. I felt that my trauma connected to the trauma of the greater world. By the end I had a vivid sense that a more global healing was pulsing through my body.

My cervix softened and opened my throat. Lower Mouth received as Upper Mouth gave. I was leaking pleasure, pain, sobs, and cum all at once, mouths releasing what they needed to in order to heal me, and each other.

An Open Letter to My Nipples

[This letter contains explicit and sensitive material – please read the author's note on pages 128–129.]

I. FIXATION
Nipples, I think about you constantly.

II. THE LET DOWN

let down *n. The release of milk in a nursing mother or lactating animal*
I had another top surgery dream last night.

In this vision, a group of friends and I had all traveled en masse to a far-off, tropical locale—not the usual Florida; maybe New Orleans?—to support a friend's top surgery. It was humid; frangipani air hung on the body. It felt magical.

The friend was laid out on a white sheet, unconscious in a way that seemed more like they were having a very sweet dream. We were all sitting in a circle in the open air around this friend while the surgeon performed the deed. We were holding sacred space; chanting; praying; smiling; singing.

The surgeon, who was genderless, also felt like a spiritual practitioner, as surgeons sometimes do. The way that they performed the top surgery was so gentle and noninvasive that the scars were barely visible afterward, and the nipples, maintaining their sensitivity, didn't have to be moved.

Everybody hung out afterwards, and there was food and costumes and dancing; it felt like a Mardi Gras,

perhaps like the Gay and Lesbian Mardi Gras of my
Australian adolescence.

It was dusk. People were drunk. There were fireflies.

I saw my former roommate there.
"I had another top surgery dream last night," I
admitted.
He smiled at me.

This is a very sweet top surgery dream, I think. Usually,
when I have top surgery dreams I am trying to breastfeed,
but all I have are drainage pumps full of milk.

I really, *really* want to breastfeed.

Sometimes, when my partner sucks on you the way he
does—gorgeous, sensuous, feminist—I feel like I want him to
keep doing it until milk, laced with oxytocin, springs from
you into his mouth. Then he and I will be bonded: like
mother and child, like kin, like lovers. This is not shameful
to me. I am kinky and I have many kinks. But I've thought
about it a lot, Nipples, and wanting to nurse is not my
kink. If anything, it is my recovery.

let down *n. A decrease in size, volume, or force*
My first boyfriend and I, and you, were 16 when we started
dating. He was my first kiss. None of us had made it past
first base before. You and I hadn't even made it to a base
before.

He was obsessed with sucking on you; remember? He
started doing it a month after we started dating—without
asking. We would make out, and then he would almost
immediately lift up my shirt and start sucking, like I were
a soda machine at an all-you-can-eat buffet. I felt sick,
dead.

This wasn't meant to be your introduction to pleasure,
Nipples.

Once I remember him doing it in public, at night, walking down a suburban street to his house. We were making out, giggling, frolicking. Then he stopped me, lifted up my shift and bra, and, to quote Bikini Kill, *sucked my left one*. Do you remember that?

Do you remember the things that happen to you?

My left breast was, and still is, smaller than the right one. I remember when, noticing this while sucking away at you, he looked up and said to me, "This one just needs a little more encouragement" and sucked on that one for longer.

I withered inside and stayed small, Nipples.

I remember when we were 17 and away at a junior national fencing competition, reuniting and reveling with teen fencers from around the country. I was hooking up with a hot female friend in front of my ex and his friend. It was for us, not them. They were just there. My ex toasted over us—as in pretended to have a glass of alcohol, or perhaps did have a glass of alcohol, and made a toasting gesture, verbally admiring the view with his friend. Something along the lines of "We've got booze, we've got a view..."

I blocked them out of my hazy, drunken mind. I was busy. My hot friend was giving me head. It was none of their business.

My ex's friend moved over to me and saw that you were exposed, erect.

He sucked on you. He did not ask me.

The next day, I told some friends. They laughed at me.

let down n. *A disappointment or a feeling of disappointment*
There was a woman I was in love with in my high school friend circle. We hooked up a couple of times back then. We haven't spoken in years, not since she moved to the east coast of Australia, leaving her history with all of us behind.

In her later teens she behaviorally fled her Christian
fundamentalist upbringing and troubled familial support
system, spiraling out into drugs and unsafe promiscuity.
She lied a lot. She clung to her arms in her sleep until
she bruised. She fucked my boyfriend/ex-boyfriend. She
hooked up with my crush in his bed while I was in the next
room, unaware and still hopeful. When I moved to the
States for college she moved in with my ex, or so I heard
years later, and they told everybody that they were in love.
And then she moved to the other side of the country to
rejoin her family and religion, getting married to a guy
who sexually assaulted her.

They have a baby now. Are they happy?

I loved sucking this woman's nipples.

One time, she stood over me and lifted up her white
singlet halfway, exposing the bottoms of her breasts. She
posed for me, tugging on her cap and miniskirt, thrusting
out her hip: a slutty cheerleader. I lifted up her shirt and
starting sucking. I didn't ask her.

Another time, at a family-and-friends-type party at
her parents' house, she had a panic attack. I followed her
upstairs to comfort her. She told me that her father, who
always unsettled me, had been sexually assaulting her. I
had many questions I didn't ask.

This scared me out of my queerness for almost a
decade.

I still have a great sexual appetite for people with
breasts, though I rarely act on it now. I theorize that I am
still too wounded from what went on before. That's part
of it, I'm sure. Mostly, though, I'm afraid to violate the
breast-havers with my desires.

I play it in my head, over and over: I see my lover's
breasts and grab them with my taking-hands, letting
all the toxic masculinity deposited onto—into—me by so

many bodies ooze out at once. My lover withers, as I did, becoming distorted and fixated too.

Maybe I was always destined to be a breast- and nipple-lover.

I drank so much breast milk from my mother that she had to pull me off her, lest I sucked her dry.

One time, when I was less than two years old, we were in the bath with her. You were tiny back then. I twisted my mother's huge nipples and cried out: "Pretty buttons!"

My first crush was Jessica Rabbit. I would stare at her breasts and get hot between my legs. I was three. I rewatched *Who Framed Roger Rabbit?* until I wore out the VHS.

As soon as I learned to draw, I would draw Disney-princess-type women in princess-cut dresses with Jessica Rabbit proportions: enormous breasts, tapered waists, blue eyes, blonde hair, massive lips, long lashes. I was an overweight "wog" girl—frizzy brown hair, big nose, double chin—and half a boy inside.

I wanted to *be* Princess Jasmine. I wanted to *fuck* Princess Jasmine. I wanted Aladdin to *fuck* me. I wanted to *be* Aladdin.

When I was seven, my friend came over and taught me how to make my Barbies make out with each other, topless, undressing each other with their plastic knife-hands—clothes getting stuck on right-angle arms—and fondling each other's nippleless breasts.

Later in the scene, I made a Ken doll assault a Barbie, and then I made Barbie take Ken to court for sexual harassment. I made my friend do Barbie's voice in the courtroom. I fed her the lines. My friend didn't want to. She was seven too.

When I was ten I saw a dance performance with my family: a dark-haired man and a blonde, statuesque woman were doing the tango. The woman looked like

Barbie. The man dipped the woman and lifted her back up; she kissed him passionately, grabbing his face with both hands. I wanted the woman to kiss me. I wanted to be the man.

III. MAGIC

Recently, a new lover fucked me without asking me. We were in bed together. Things escalated. I couldn't find my "No." I cried the next day. He listened.

Before the fucking, this person told me that my breasts were "magic," because he sucked on you, Nipples, and I had an orgasm.

I'm still amazed by your superpower. You give me orgasms. *Nipplegasms.*

And you know what? My breasts *are* magic. Pendulous, soft, and creased with colorless stretch marks, with huge alveoli and a hair or two around the edge. They hang heavy, and taper beautifully into the soft points of you. They are gorgeous. *You* are gorgeous, and you are *highly* responsive. You give me orgasms. You are magic.

IV. DESIRE

This was what I masturbated to as a horny sixteen-year-old with a nipple fixation:

Fantasy #1: Coming into my hot 34-year-old high-school teacher's office and begging for an A. Opening my uniform (a colonial-chic navy Aboriginal-print dress with a tie) to reveal my pert teenage breasts. We make out. I put his hand on my right breast and he fondles me. I guide his head toward you, Nipples, and he sucks on you. Then the principal is about to come into his office. I hide under his desk, which has an opening for legs but is opaque otherwise. He sits at his desk, hiding me from the open side, and bids the principal enter. I unzip his fly and suck his dick to climax while he speaks with the principal, barely stifling his pleasure. I greedily suck his semen down.

Semen is a bit like breast milk, don't you think?

Fantasy #2: I am a journalist covering an event at the Playboy mansion. I have on a black pencil skirt with matching garter stockings and pointy black pumps. My white sheer blouse reveals a sexy black bra, with matching high-cut, black lacy underwear.

The Playboy bunnies are wearing outfits that look like black bathing suits with holes to let their gravity-defying breasts poke through. The holes and edges of the suits are laced with white doily fabric. They look like French maid bunnies.

One of the bunnies is assigned to me as a tour guide. She is sexy, and looks like a cast member of *Baywatch*. I take a tour of the mansion and grounds. Finally, I am led through a series of underwater grottos. We pass another Playboy bunny straddling a man, squatting on his dick and riding him wildly and he lay flat on his back, receiving, helpless to her desire. They are both fully clothed except for his dick and her breasts and cunt. The bunny suit has another hole, it seems. They moan and scream with nasty, opulent pleasure, fucking away in that damp, gray grotto on the cold, stone ground, splayed out next to a shimmering swimming pool bathed in light from a skylight overhead. My bunny leads me nonchalantly past them, shooting me a coy glance as I stare. In the next grotto, a tall waterfall tumbles lustily into a lagoon. My bunny asks me if I've seen enough, if there's anything more that I'll be wanting from her. Am I interested in what I saw? Curious? She takes me behind the waterfall so that nobody can see. She is soaking wet. She puts my face onto her breast to suck. I suck her nipples. Then she sucks mine: you.

I am masturbating and touching, pinching, *twisting* you as I write this.

V. REMOVAL

My obsession with breast removal, breast sucking, and breast*feeding* are all parallel, as in *they do not touch.*

I remember a sixth-grade classmate giving a speech about Amazon women and how they cut off their left breasts. I was eleven. I returned to this image for a long time. I later learned that it was to better shoot with a bow and arrow. *What about the lefties?*

One time in eighth grade: I was rifling through a glossy magazine, and I saw a slender, modelesque woman with buzzed blonde hair and almost no makeup, wearing a singlet that clearly showed a flat chest. The caption read that she didn't want her breasts anymore, so she removed them. I wonder where this person is now. Who is she? Is she trans? Was this article woefully gender incompetent, or did she still use she/her pronouns at the time of her surgery? Why did I fixate on this image for so long?

For years after my experiences with my first boyfriend, I saw and felt dark energy in my right breast, the larger one. The one that needed less "encouragement."

My first energy healer told me that I needed to sort out my relationship with my breasts. She saw the dark energy too. She saw that I sometimes wanted them gone.

My transmasc friends tell me that one can lose sensation in one's nipples after top surgery. This prospect *horrifies* me.

Once, when I was 20, I cried about not being a man. I was in the arms of my gay male friend, in college, in bed. It was late. He kissed me. I cried some more. Then I got up and put on mascara. Or was the mascara another time?

One of my greatest sexual appetites is for queer men who fuck other queer men. They don't see the queer man in me.

I met a beautiful 53-year-old transman last year. He was a radical faerie, and had transitioned seven years ago. He had always been butch, and was always attracted to queer and gay men. He had sex with men before his transition but "it never felt right." Now it feels right. He told me that he underwent the physical transformation so that people would see him for who he was, so that he could have sex with the people to whom he was attracted. It wasn't as much for himself, I don't think.

I highly identify with this story.

Maybe when I am middle-aged, and done breastfeeding, I will transform into a queer man and have sex with the faeries for the rest of my life.

VI. HYBRID

I have worked with the same energy healer for the past five years now. Her name is Eva. Many miracles, too many to name here, have occurred as a result of my work with her. One stands out: The dark energy is gone from my breasts now. I am very kind to them. I am still confused by them, sometimes, by their existence on my chest, but I accept their presence in my life as long as they are there. *You* will always be there, Nipples.

Eva helped me recover my gender too. I am a *hybrid*. Like the car; like a mule; like an orchid.

Dear Torso,

Built like a Donkey Kong barrel flung down stairs. Jump over them to save the princess. A ribcage is supposed to be smaller than that. Narrow your shoulders. Big breasts are unseemly on such a large frame. It feels like you spill everywhere. To be loved you must be contained.

Dear Torso, I'm sorry that I told you that I needed to be the perfect woman before I could be anything else, that I ever thought that queer was my personal cop out for never feeling pretty. I felt like I needed to be (not feel, but be) pretty before I could wear boy shoes (size 6.5, that aisle still makes me nervous) or cutting my hair short or saying please don't call me a fucking woman for the love of god stop having me fill out my gender on paperwork. I felt like I needed to ask my ribcage to please pull in more, curl into that cavity if you must. From the side it should only be tits past the arm. It's not even about that flat stomach.

Be woman be woman be woman

Is that why you slept with so many men, who you like sometimes but – oh boy – not in those cases?

It's about narrowness, about a fine form from the back, not wide shoulders leading in a tube of tummy and hips.

Dear Torso, sorry that I wished you were a different shape. Sorry that I feel like someone took the photoshop tool and dragged you a few clicks bigger than the rest of me. (Hips down is fine.)

Not quite sculpted right for that final (for now at least) reveal of my not womanhood, sometimes manhood, mainly dad on vacation miniskirt self that felt like the final nail in the coffin of what I was supposed to be.

To My Boy Parts:

I'm sorry we hadn't really met before I shoved you back inside me. I didn't even know you existed before that terrible kitchen floor, and you were peeking out, trying to make yourself known. "Hey, you know you're sometimes a girl, and you suspect sometimes you're nothing, but did you know that you're sometimes a boy, too?!" You were so honest, so trusting. I was so trusting. I let her into my life. I shared my fantasies with her. But my fantasies hadn't counted on you. You were a guest, a newcomer, a surprise attraction. She was counting on my submissive female desires. My fighting back should have told her to stop, but we hadn't talked about safe words and warning signs. She fucked the boy right back inside me.

I blocked you out. I couldn't deal with admitting my trusted girlfriend had raped me. Even now it's hard to write, but even harder to think. I automatically shut down, make my mind blank. I squared my jaw and comforted her when she realized she had done wrong. She cried on my shoulder and I dealt with it, (ironically enough), like a man.

I went back to "normal". Back to girl and girlfriend. Back to trying to make "lesbian" work, before understanding the beauty of the word "queer." I eventually revisited the non-binary parts of me. Through theatre and acting, I found the genderqueer trans pieces that fit after characters I played seemed closer to me in their in-betweenness than anyone else I had portrayed.

But I assumed I'd always hang out in the middle. Neither boy nor girl. I was certain "genderqueer" was right because "gender fluid" implies bouncing from male to female, masculine to feminine. I thought I was directly in the middle. I felt in-between.

I know now it's from pushing you away.

I'm getting better. I still like "genderqueer," but I do have boy days now. Sometimes my spouse (a better, more communicating partner than the one who betrayed us), encourages me to re-discover you; to be a boy. During the day or the night. In bed or out of it. I can connect there with my brain, but my body still tenses and shuts down. My boy still hides. My body isn't there yet. My boy parts aren't there yet.

I don't know if you're a penis or not. I hadn't fully met you before I shoved you back inside me. But I'm ready when you are.

Take your time.

But I'm ready.

you are sweet to me occasionally.

You were unlike many accounts I read in the vagina monologue. Stupidly I thought the lack of relation I had for what you were before, would become relation to what you had become. No such luck. None at all. I thought that all the pains and bruises wouldn't transfer either. You were my new lovely vagina. Shine from between my legs, filling up the room with your brilliant splendor but it did.

It did.

The pain transfered.

The rape I experience had nothing to do with this right? That happened before your loveliness was born. You were free from that past. This was your beginning. I thought I could run away and forgot it all. It didn't scar you, it was me. And in the beginning you weren't a part of me. It was my fondest hopes that such joy and happiness would pour out of you so sweet and gooey like milk and honey. But so far all that came out was pain and with that pain was a reminder of past pain. Even if you looked so perfect in the mirror. Even if your reflection made you feel so complete.

I wasn't complete. I wasn't.

There wasn't any milk or any honey. You weren't sweet at first. No you weren't. As you were birthed into this world screaming. "Owww, this motherfucking shit hurts!" You made me question my whole identity. I wonder if I made the right choice. And because of how you made me feel at first, I hated you.

And then you healed.

And you started to feel better and you give me pleasure,
that before made me feel shame. Now it was just pleasure,
seeping pleasure. Pleasure that I didn't let myself
experience before because it was connected to so much
shame. But now it's only connected to just pleasure. I am
still scared to touch you. I am careful of who I let meet
you. I don't want to upset you. Everyone tells me I am crazy,
when I say I don't want to break you. I still haven't figured
you out yet and that's ok.

Untitled

Dear Hair,

Thank you for your boldness. You always bounce back
– nothing can tame your curls or bleach your color.
Thank you for the fluidity you grant me, for how you are
feminine, masculine, and everything in between. You
remind me to stay true to myself.

Dear Voice,

Thank you for coming back. You've been strong and patient
as I re-learn how to communicate – how to say how I
feel, what I want, and what I need in relationships. Thank
you for helping me speak up. For overflowing with truth,
laughter, and song.

Dear Breasts,

What can I thank you for? What have I leaned from you?
You taught me about vulnerability and shame through
harsh, sharp experience. I pushed against his chest, crying.
"Why won't you show me your breasts? Are you ashamed of
them?" As I put my bra back on, I thought that I must hate
my breasts if I couldn't show them to him. My twelve-year-
old mind didn't realize that I wasn't ready – that it was
okay to be young, vulnerable, and soft. It was the first time
I hardened myself. Thank you for staying soft.

Dear Legs,

You are my strength. You are the hard to my femme. You
are my Polish plow-girl legs, my tree trunks rooting me
into the earth. Every hair, sun speckle, scar, scabbed over
bugbite, and tattoo is exactly where it should be. You've
been through a lot a lot. I store my tension in you. You
were the first place he grabbed when he dragged me
towards him and held me down. Thank you for learning
to kick. For taking me where I need to go. For refusing to
give up.

Dear Vagina,

Thank you for your resilience. After the assaults, after
the years of silent, painful sex, after being taught that
your only use was someone else's pleasure, you shine. You
radiate warmth, you come over, and over, and over, every
orgasm reminding me that I am resilient, strong, and
worthy of love.

Dear Brain,

When I first learned what trauma does to the brain, how
it carves new pathways into the soft gray flesh, I felt
defeated. I thought that my abusers had won, that I was
irreversibly damaged. Then I realized that plasticity works
both ways. That every time I go to therapy, have a long talk
with a friend, realize something about myself, feel safe
in someone else's arms, use my voice, and remember to
breathe, I am shaping my own brain, like a steady flow of
water gently carving a new landscape.

Let it flow,
Let it flow,
Let it flow.

Dear tender squishy wonderful belly,

The last person who assaulted me tried to convince me that you were wrong. "You are the fattest girl I've ever been with." Like he deserved a medal. "I actually think you'd be hot if you lost ten pounds." Cool. "I'm still attracted to you though." We didn't shut him up. We didn't know how. He didn't get you. He couldn't see me. We didn't want to be seen. We didn't know how.

Sweet belly, when I first found femme I learned to love you better. To see your curves as essential to my being. And as femme fits less or not less but less often less always, I know I need to do more work to love you. So. As my gender changes [[in response in healing in survival in resistance in refusal in who knows what]] I am here telling you I will do the work. I will let you grow with me.

A week ago, I noticed new stretch marks tiger striped on your underside. Who knows how long they'd been there, hidden from me, visible to anyone lucky enough to get that view. I wish I'd known sooner. I wish I'd been the first to know. I wish I could kiss them. Messy belly, I want to give you more attention. I've been touching those marks every day since I saw them and whispering softly I love you. I love you.

And I would like that to be true. If I'm honest, which I like to be, I don't believe myself when I say I love you. It's not a lie, but it's ambitious. I don't trust myself to love you. I don't trust my body. I don't trust the people who hold you, kiss you, slap you fondly to love you either. To get to know you. To love me. To get to know me. Even when they touch you and whisper softly. Even then. Still.

Still, fat fat belly, you remind me I am soft. That I can be soft. That soft is not weak. That soft carries weight. Soft is I've had enough else to know I'd like to try being tender. Soft is connection. Soft is conversation. Soft is hard for me. There are reasons bugs crawl belly down. There are reasons we keep our tender spots hidden.

And soft is femme. But not only. Dear belly, I worry with you [[with me with my body]], I can't be seen outside of femininity. Not that I always want to. I worry I'm betraying myself, overcomplicating what I somehow should fit into. Dear belly, you don't fit. Dear belly, you have never fit. Into clothes my mother bought me I wasn't allowed to choose, stares in the locker room, or rapist boys' expectations. I was never allowed this body as it is. This body has never belonged to me. Dear belly, you belong. Dear belly, I think I do love you. I think so. Dear belly, I will tell them to kiss you. To get tangled in your mess of hair. To be so sweet with you. I will be sweet with you. I will tell them they can't be scared of you. I want to be less scared of you. I want to be less scared.

Breathe deeply. Feel you expand. Feel you grow. Hold you. Hold on. And thank you. Thank you. Thank you.

To my fifteen-year-old chest,

I'm... I'm... I'm speechless. Which is a pretty common occurrence for me, actually. It's just that there are so many things that I want to say, that I can't get them out fast enough so they just get stuck or they end up coming out in a jumbled mess, like subway riders on a rush hour train with their thrashing shoulders and dirty looks.

It's just that I'm sorry. I'm sorry that you had to go, but for as long as I've known you, I knew you weren't for me. I love you on other people, I really do. And it's not even a, "it's not you, it's me," kinda thing, because it's neither of our faults. And you were objectively great – functional, beautiful – everything someone else wants and deserves, I'm sure.

And I'm sorry that I didn't stick up for you more. Like when all the band guys embarrassed you and teased you for being too perky, when you were just cold. From then on, I wore a few layers everyday so you wouldn't get leered at. I don't know if you noticed, but that was for you. And, like, when I fell asleep in Christa's basement and woke up to Dave's greasy hands up my shirt, touching you and grabbing you. I can't tell you what I was thinking, because I don't think I was. I was just paralyzed and pretending to still be asleep, until I rolled over and he had to pull his hand away.

I've tried to stop apologizing so much recently, and instead say thank you. I think you do deserve those apologies, but I also want to say thank you. Would my life be easier if I'd never known you? If my chest had stayed flat through puberty and if I didn't have to wear these scars everyday

as evidence that you were here? Maybe, sure. Would my
life be better if I'd never known you? No, I don't think
so. Easier is not always better. I'm so glad you and I were
brought together, because you helped me learn so much
about other people, and so much about myself. Going
through a struggle always produces a new perspective,
like that stupid metaphor about diamonds forming under
pressure.

I have the honor of being a special kind of human, and I'm
grateful that I knew you on my journey.

Love,

Dear Hair,

In youth, never did you flee from shears, shirk from snippers. Never did you shiver in fright at being trimmed into submission before church. Men on the street said you resembled Heidi or Laura Ingalls with two long braids. You were evidence that my mother loved wild. She would not repeat authoritarian mistakes. You let her convince herself, "I'm a good mom to my daughter. I let her be free."

People talked to you more than me. Isn't it heavy? How do you wash it? What do you use? Do you get split ends? Can you braid it yourself? Then, later, Can I touch it? It's turning me on. Would you use the tip to tickle my chest? I think I'm gonna cum.

We replace our skin every seven years. You remain unchanged. You held early memories of the smell of bleach and weed at your tips. Then an inch for crying. An inch for blanket tents. An inch for yelling. An inch for empty beer bottles. An inch for stuffing socks in my pants. An inch for black candles and curses. Once I measured you at four feet precisely. Four feet of shame.

Did you tremble when, after 33 years of growing unencumbered, I set up the video camera in Dad's bathroom and slid the shears from their sheath? You look overgrown and brambly in the documentary, a thicket between me, the Prince, from me, the Beauty. I snip you tenderly at first, as though it will be an amicable divorce, then abandon the plan and hack indiscriminately. You're like the hydra, sending out fresh shoots the more I cut off. You're lopsided, incorrigible, spiraling, sprung from the trap of your own weight.

Four hours later, we recover from the ordeal. You part
to let air fondle my scalp, lascivious breeze. I see a face
peering out from the mirror, framed by your asymmetrical
jaunt: hard jaw, dilated eyes, pink lips. You look surprised.
The dismembered parts of you don't seem to mind being
tangled on the floor, swept into a blanket, and buried in
the yard.

You lied. You said I'd cry. You said I had so much to lose.
You said I'd never go through with it. I'd be ugly and
plain, another brown, brown-haired lump slogging along,
defeminized. I'd never have the guts. Ha! But I catch
you showing off, now and then, with a spike, a daring
sideburn. And what do I say when a queerdo stops me on
the train, "I like your haircut!"

I say, "Thanks! I cut it myself."

Letter to My Body Hair

She wanted me to grow you. Before she was she, before I was they, before a time when she yelled at me whenever I wanted to share the pictures from our wedding, when we were a bride and groom, however non-traditional everything else might have been. She liked hairy girls. When she broke up with me and I let someone equally obsessed with my copious amounts of body hair go down on me without a dental dam, she tried to tell me I had done something wrong. My body was hers, even when she didn't want it.

I was embarrassed about you, and I was proud of you. Once, pre-HRT, a friend looked at my legs in shorts and asked me if I was on testosterone. No, I laughed, recently socially transitioned and secretly so happy that someone thought I was medically transitioning. I'm Italian. Once, a man in the street called me it, pointing to my legs in shorts, adding that he thought it was a dude. You made me look so queer, heightened my non-binaryness to almost everyone. You were also the thing that made me a target outside my little bubble of queerness.

She made me okay with you, when I never had been before. It was a gift, in a way, to understand my own self, my own body, to have someone give you love when I could not. Isn't that always the foundation for what came later? You were also a gift for her, one she didn't demand but pressed for, making me think it was best for me. That was the way with everything she wanted. When things changed I looked at you wondering who you belonged to.

I remember that moment—the last moment, though I wouldn't realize it for a year, until I sat in an office with her and my therapist, saying the words, "This is worse than the time you sexually assaulted me"—the way her semen glistened in you, and I stood up to go to the bathroom, to wipe it off, to fumble around for the day-after contraceptive I knew I needed to take. So many times I had parted you, put in the diaphragm she insisted I use, that she knew I hated. She hated condoms, they were so much worse for her dysphoria than diaphragms were for mine. Nevermind that a condom was off after sex, and a diaphragm was something I held in my body for a dozen hours of panic. Her needs were always the most important. That was why I acquiesced, finally, saying, "We'll do it without contraceptives, but don't cum in me." She couldn't even respect that. She came in and on me.

After, she said, "I just raped you, didn't I?" After, she wrote a song about her feelings.

I forgave her. Isn't that always the foundation for what came later? How she convinced everyone I had abused her? How everyone believed her, because she was the woman, because I was masc, because why would I have stayed with her if that's what she'd really done?

You were hers. You grew because of her desires. What other purpose could you have than to glisten with her?

It took me two years to shave you off and start again.

hands

you begin to do
such delicate things
to such delicate people
and doesn't it feel
like licking thick fire
out of the batter-bowl

To my voice,

I'm afraid of you becoming a wolf.

I'm afraid of the scratching, the bark of his voice that made me lock my bedroom door. Reliving my howl of the nights I told myself I would rather die than be a boy who can do those things that I know boys can do.

For years you sang me lullabies and hymns, anything to make us soften before the impending attack, the hound who hounded my body.

You could never stop him, Voice, your huff and puff caught under his quickening growl. You became so tired, in the third grade I set you free. You played dead, gone far, far too long. I could hardly think of you as a part of my body because you could not protect it.

Will hormones, your deepening into my soul turn you foul or rabid? Will your familiarity trick the rest of me into thinking he's inside the house again? The wolf dressed as a loved one just to get inside.

If one day you deepen, grow hair on every limb, sounding like a wolf, please don't eat the rest of us within. Never forget, Voice, why you ran away to begin with.

Yours,

Dear Neck,

I'm sorry they tried to break you. I'm sorry they grabbed
you and wrung you with their dirty calloused hands. I'm
sorry that they ever got to touch you. I'm sorry I never
let you hold my head as high as I should have because I
was too scared to look them in the eye. I'm sorry the hurt
went on for so long. But I hope you know I love you and
I'm grateful for the way you rest my head at night and the
way your hairs stand up when a lover whispers in my ear.
I hope you feel comforted by warm scarves and coffee in
the winter. I hope you feel beautiful in jewelry and silk ties.
Most of all I hope you feel loved and every much a part of
my body as the rest of me.

Thank you.

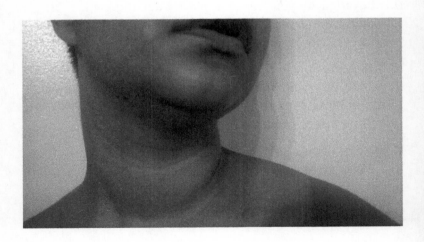

Letter to the Bags under My Eyes

Are you tired?
You look tired.
Why do you always look so tired?

Hi, misplaced blood. Hey, bruise-colored crescents. How are you, twin stains below my vision? How's it been?

I know you don't come from lack of sleep – I know better. You come from dust, from pollen, every small invasion that my body can't handle. My allergies are a force, tearing through my face with mucous and water. The kids at school used to make fun of me for sneezing when I was younger, named me a secondhand dwarf, not small enough to make my roundness inoffensive. Even now, better medicated and away from a histamine house, you persist, a stormcloud reminder that it might rain.

When I get tired, the color washes out of my face and I'm more likely to cry. You darken alongside those symptoms even though you don't belong to them. I know what it's like to have to move with what's around you. I'm allergic to my basement, whether to the carpet or the memories I can't tell. Sometimes there's a swelling and you don't know why. You just know you have to leave.

When people ask you how you are, you're supposed to lie. Fine, good, can't complain, like flesh-colored concealer over your darkened places. During the slow drowning of my early twenties, I found a way to skirt the lie. Said "I'm tired" instead of "I'm getting straight As and in my nightmares I kiss a boy who tried to devour me and when I wake up a new love is filling me with poison." Instead of "I don't feel worthy unless I'm needed." Instead of "help me."

How are you?
I'm tired.

What happened to you?
I'm tired.

Are you a boy or a girl?
I'm tired.

My trauma is tired, weary of being trotted out as an excuse or wielded like a tool to make cis men rethink situations they assume they understand. My gender is tired, womanhood worn down to a femme blur that wavers at the edges. I'm tired of having to explain both before I understand them myself. I'm tired of each day being a reaction and not a creation.

I react to my body, to the swelling, to the running, to every discolored reminder that there have been invasions here. I waver at the edges. I carve a list of flaws into my reflection, and you are so often top of the list.

I react to what is put onto my body – womanhood, victimhood, any other heavy thing drawn over my face to keep me from seeing. I take it in. Let it refract through the holes in me till it looks like truth. Even though my body protests, puffs and discolors an unwelcome.

You aren't a martyr or a metaphor. You're a reminder, that my body reacts to the unseen. That unseen is not invisible, is not imaginary. Is mine. Something I deserve to know for myself. But that's what's around you – when I look at you, you're small. Two half-moons the size of knuckles, and I have whole hands. Hands that can build a ladder out of shame, can tie shoelaces on feet walking new ground.

I carry my past in my body, and I carry my body forward. To new ground, to a future that won't be all balm or all burden. But I'll be there for it: awake. Eyes open, leading the rest of me. I don't want to end with closure that isn't real – I don't want to end. We have a ways to go, you and I. There is so much left to heal from. To create together. There is so much more to see.

I love you.

patchwork

(i). i try to grasp at your silk-woven heart, my heart beats faster than your hands do. always at work, both always at war: the connections between hands to wrists to elbows to release: the same joints join up to make your armour. we clank & shatter together with the flow & ebb of some tide & i am empty once more. but you are ready: cardamon & هدوء & dates & almonds pad me out; fill my holes. bulge out of me. the blankness of my eyes is milky white for a reason.

> these things sustain me & keep me whole. i eat
> not for life but for hope.

(ii). my seams are stitched up with the thread of despair [it was too thick to go through the eye of the needle properly so that is why i am loose in myself]. i shake a lot which does not help.

> needles taunt me because they only need one eye to
> witness beauty & i need both but am
> blind in one. no amount of milk can fix that.

(iii). the crevices between my joints are the weakest part of me. they crease when all i do is look at them [i look at them often]. it is so hard for me to hold myself together. i am scared of the way my skin brushes my bones & i can never find the pulse on my wrist. i did not ask for this. i did not ask.

(iv). my legs have lost mass since i started walking back from death. the small mounds on my chest serve as a reminder that people want me to go back.

my mother. she held the thread. she made me this way & is
sad i don't thank her.

(v). so i sit by her legs & press her feet & am grateful she
makes me hurt. i do not know my mother. she thinks i am
someone who constantly wants to feel hot breath down
my neck.

i think she is blessed.

i do not know my mother, even if she is usually good with
thread.

**[i need someone i know to stitch me back up
properly but everyone i know is rubbish at sewing]**

the crevices between my joints are the cleanest parts of me
& still they are bruised. shades darker than our knuckles, i
am a shaken, dust-ridden quiltbag; punch me & yes, i did
ask. (without the questions, i would be more air than the
rush, the adrenaline that propels you to fight, to always
fight. i always *float*).

(vi). i wear clothes that hide the marks & have decided to
take matters into my own hands;
although trembling is their natural state, they do a good
job of seeking out finer & finer thread:

i have tried pulling out hair
i have tried unraveling the past
i have tried plucking at grief
& there is more to come. there is more to come.

(vii). sometime i run out of almonds
or the milk doesn't taste as sweet
or the date stones
catch on to my lining
reminding me that i will always be wrongly bound:
i am told to go back & perhaps i should
for at least موت could tie me to the ground.

Dear Body,

I am sorry.

You have been through so much. You have felt the
struggles of my brain as it played tug of war with your
parts. Placing things here and there, pulling them this
way and that, trying to figure out what you wanted to be
until finally landing on that perfect spot in the middle.
Queer, I call you. Not man. Not woman. But something in
between. Genderqueer. The first time I heard that word I
could not think fast enough. Something that described me.
Something that described this body. Sixteen-year-old me
was ecstatic. I read up on you as much as I could. Blogs
on MySpace. Random websites. Anything that showed up
on Google. I had a word for you. The clothes shifted as I
learned more and became comfortable. I dressed you in
tight jeans and baggy hoodies, skirts, even a dress once
or twice. I never told anyone how great it felt to be in
my first dress. It was a dare. Seventeen-almost-eighteen-
year-old me at a party in my basement. And by party I
mean a group of about 10 of my friends playing truth or
dare and spin the bottle completely sober. Because we
were straight edge then. We got a dare. To change clothes
with our friend Jessica. Her pink and white striped dress
fit us perfect. It fell to our knees and stuck to our skin
and I felt great. Coming out of the basement workroom
in that dress was like opening the curtain to a brand
new show on Broadway. The audience was excited and
supportive and kept screaming. We beamed. And quickly
went and changed in case Mom came down to see what we
were doing.

No one knew about the struggle we were facing. That struggle that came with every meal around others. That struggle of what was enough or too much or what needed to be avoided altogether. You did not break 100 lbs until sophomore year. All I remember thinking after that was that I needed to stay there. I needed to stay at that number and I shouldn't go higher. When we moved away to college, things changed. I was surrounded by strength, by support, and by people who would come to love me even more than I thought possible. This struggle began to wane as I worked through it, moving forward with my love for you. Realizing that you were something great and not just a number on the scale.

Until he came along. He loved the way you were. Loved the way your ribs stuck out at the side. Loved how small you felt in his hands. Loved the way people would misgender you for a cisgendered girl. And I loved him. As the months went by his words broke down any recovery that we had built. I'm sorry. He tore down the support beams and everything came crashing down. We avoided eating around people and when we did eat around people we didn't eat for the rest of the day. That magic number jumped around as every time we would get it low he would say, "Wow, you look so sexy." His attraction to us was directly tied to that number and all I wanted was his attraction to us and I am sorry.

Trying to be active came at a cost. The starving body I was trying to call home did its best to hold me up but every time I fell another part of you broke.

My wrist.

Fractured.

My knee.

Bruised.

My collarbone.

Fractured.

My self esteem.

Destroyed.

After mere months of being with him he began taking his frustrations for the world out on you. The corner of the filing cabinet pierced your back as you fell that first time he hit you. Those knives felt so sharp every time he threatened you with their points. The bleach smelt so strong as he tried to pour it all over the clothes that adorned you. The ground felt...so hard when he would tackle you to it. His rage was hard to measure. We could never be sure when he was about to snap. So we tried to please him.

He made our identity into nothing but a fetish. Seeing the skirts and dress and tight clothes he saw a sex object. An object that he could control and use. He always asked us to wear certain things for him. And controlled the way we could look. Some days I would go to plug in that straightener only to find it missing. Some days I would look for that makeup to accentuate you and make me feel better only to find out we were leaving now and he was not waiting. My identity was his to toy with. Only when he wanted me to would I be able to be my authentic self. Meeting his friends he controlled how I looked. Wearing his ex's hoodie, my hair greasy and not done, wearing glasses instead of contacts, my face make up less, my pants a size too big held up with a belt, I felt the farthest from myself.

We have struggled through so much together, body. And I am sorry for the struggle you have gone through. The bruises we hid with concealer and long hair. With clothes that covered my body. With questions unanswered. With concerns brushed off and ignored. With excuses.

I hope you can forgive me. I hope that you know that I love you. That I am realizing just how much we are worth. I am realizing that you may not be perfect but you are perfect for me. You and I together can move through this world in a fluid image, reflecting the identities surrounding us and creating our own. He cannot hold us back anymore.

We are free.

To the back of my neck,

You always taught me how to close. My body a castle
door against every battering ram. Loud breath but no air
striding down your hallway. Alarms sounding in every
tendon. We like to remember it as a siege. Arrows sticking
out of shoulder blades like feathers. We wanted to sing.
Scream. We wanted to fly. No kind of bird, no kind of
warrior against metal teeth. The truth is it was no siege.
Was a body and a body. A breath stealing mine. No sound.
Scream trapped in a river of his sweat. Drowning. The
truth is no wall can stop water, water was made to wear
down. Like fear.

Every time I move to soften, you unearth the dead. A panic
pantomime. Reenactment so I don't get foolish or forgiving.
You curse me for dreaming. I dream of swimming in a new
kind of river. Of a mouth, giving. You think I can't protect
us, no kind of warrior against an enemy as everywhere as
water. You, my trigger-finger love. You, killing us to save
us. You, tense. A wall between us and oxygen, and peace.
Until I give the damage its due.

I do. I read it on every page of our body. I can't forget
/ I wouldn't want to. But safety is not the same as joy. I
unbrick my wounds. I hope in a half-whisper, dip a pinkie
toe in. I want to breathe so deeply I exhale a new chapter.
One where I am still, always, grateful to you. One where I
teach you how to open.

organ donor

when i turned sixteen my license didn't have the mark of
an organ donor
back then, i saw my organs as one of the few things left as
everything was getting worse
they kept me warm at night
i was selfish

during the five years i had to think about it, i wanted to
give them away so bad
the path to my uterus had been marred by you, and my
brain stewed in your callous remarks
i would do anything to change my status
i was selfish

when i turned twenty-one my license proudly displayed
the mark
my organs mean something now
my heart can give love as fierce as a dam bursting, and my
lungs breathe in pure air
no longer selfish

when i move on
and all i can offer that is that which is tangible
i hope that you – whoever you are
will take my organs, paint the night with them, kiss the
trees, and love just like me

When I first thought about writing this letter, I was unsure to which parts of me I should be writing to. I have had weird and, at times, troubling relationships with many of them. Also, this hesitation of not knowing what will come of it. The insecurities that I think a lot of us face when we pour out our souls in vulnerable magic.

I reflected... On the things, the ways, in which hurt had come to my body, and spirit.

And... I'm sorry.

There were times when you hurt a lot physically.

When I made you, stomach, empty yourself again...and again...and again. All in the pursuit of a thinness. As growing up, I was shamed for my weight, reminded that as a "girl" my only worth was my form. Of course, not exactly worded like that. But in the commenting on my food choices, the reminding me that I "could say no to desserts," their own obsession with unattainable thinness, the dieticians. All because I was a slightly chubby kid with chronic illness. I'm sorry.

To my hands, as the blade grazed your skin again, and again...and again. And the greatest betrayal; it was my other hand doing this cruel work. As my, now ex, partner was in the other room. She didn't do it to me; but her words guided the blade, as they played in my head.

And later in the relationship, as I reached in to stop her doing this same act to herself, her hands did guide the blade across my skin. And then held the knife to the throat as she ripped me apart with her words. I'm sorry.

My ass and thighs, I've had a difficult relationship with you. My curviness often denies how I relate to my gender.

I feel like it can be a betrayal that leads people to call me she, when I'm actually they.

I do value how you hold my body so well, and, at times, appreciate your shape, and warmth, and softness, and firmness. But other times, I feel frustrated. I think sometimes relationships have conflicting feelings. we will work through it.

To my uterus... Oh...to my uterus. I dislike when you send me once a month messages in a rush of crimson. I dislike how it deeply affects my mood, my perception of my self. The drowning dysphoria. How seeing blood drip between my legs can hurt for a multitude of reasons.
Trust me, I'm all for period positivity.
But for me, it isn't a positive experience.

To my entire body. The areas that have been dehumanized and violated. Sometimes with words or glances. And sometimes, in action. Those that saw you as a body to use, not to respect. You have received cruelty at times, but also magic. You are magic.

To my body.
All of it.
Our relationship is kinda beautiful...and kinda ugly.
I love you.

NOTE TO SELF

Write or draw a letter to your own body parts here:

SINCERELY

by Sawyer DeVuyst

T he words in these pages, whether meticulously crafted
together or exorcised and spewed in fury, are complex.
Complex in their hurt, their fragility, their gratefulness,
their strength, their love, and their longing. These stories
are complex in that they're unique and they're the same.

This collection of words creates a space where there wasn't
space before. It fosters acknowledgement of the pain,
hurt, and anger that the world burdens us with. It fosters
acknowledgement of our desire, necessity, and capacity to
heal. It fosters community, in that we can feel less alone.

All I've ever wanted was to feel less alone. I grew up in
the lower half of the middle of four kids, in a born-again
Assemblies of God family, low-income in a wealthy area
outside of New York City. I wasn't allowed to have play
dates with kids from school because they weren't Christian.
I was teased at church because we were poor, my tangled
hair, second-hand clothes and plastic sneakers from
discount stores an easy target. My mounting boyishness
became a point of contention.

When I was seven, my sister was born, and my mom's
postpartum depression made it impossible for her to
function, let alone keep track of four kids. I was often left
at school for hours after everyone had left. This is no one's

fault, except a broken system that shames people with mental illness into not seeking help. But the feeling of abandonment is still living inside of me, 25 years later. The dangerous levels of self-reliance, of not asking for help, of isolating because of lack of trust are all still there, 25 years later. They rear their head when I'm alone, in my romantic relationships, and in my friendships. Growing up, I'd never been asked what my needs were—what my wants were—so I never learned to ask for them.

I came out as transgender eight years ago, and it has taken me almost all eight of those years to firstly, settle into my identity as an agender person, and secondly, to realize this: We are more alike than we are different. There are so many ways of being. Of being human, of being trans, of being queer, of being survivors. But the core of who we are as humans, of what we want as humans, binds us together. We all want to be seen and accepted and cherished as we are. As ourselves. As. Our. Selves. Trans people are often told flat-out (or backhandedly) that we're less-than, that we're undeserving of care, of employment, of housing, of safety, of love. Personally, I've been told to my face that I'm disgusting, I'm an abomination, I'm unnatural, I will become a pedophile, I'm disfiguring my body, that I'm ruining my life, that my family will be ashamed of me. Based on nothing else other than my transness.

While dating a woman I loved for seven years, it was impossible for me to vocalize what I needed and wanted. And after telling her that I was trans, I didn't have the tools to navigate conversations about what that meant for me, for her, for us. It was one of the most isolating times in my life, and I truly felt like I had no one to turn to who would understand.

When chronic uniqueness, the feeling that I am the only person experiencing a problem or hardship, has threatened to overwhelm me, hearing stories of the human condition have saved me. Hearing stories from other people about how others have treated them, how it made them feel, how they overcame it, or how they sat with those feelings, make me feel less alone. It has created a community of "I see you. I hear you."

This anthology creates a community of "I see you. You see me. I hear you. You hear me. I feel you. You feel me." It creates a space where we are all valid and free to feel, without judgement or expectations. I hope this community—this space—is somewhere we can all feel whole.

PPS, AN AFTERWORD

by Lexie Bean

I was once asked, "Why don't you write about something else?"

I think she was trying to protect me, and/or protect herself.

It was just a week before I was planning to start collecting letters for this book. I wondered whether I was doing a selfish thing, or if I would be writing my future away. I'm learning that neither of these things are true.

This project began in 2012 when I was in the neurology ward of a hospital in Budapest, Hungary. It's easy to say I was there because I contracted a virus. It's true, I did have a virus, but I went to the hospital simply because my body was too tired to fight it. The two weeks leading up to my visit to the emergency room, life piled up: eating disorders resurfaced in my family, there were talks of a restraining order, a dear friend of mine was murdered, I said hello and goodbye to a girl I was very much in love with. Throughout college, I fell into the habit of going to hospitals to find an easy word to describe impossible feelings, alongside an easy cure for them.

I needed something inside to say, "Stop running, stop running, you can stay here." That summer I wrote to my leg hair and my hymen. I couldn't write about something else. There were too many pieces I was trying to bring back to my body. No one is selfish for offering themselves a place to stay.

Coming out as trans has complicated, for me, what it means to make house in my own body. I made this anthology to combat one of my biggest fears: that physically transitioning will make me look more and more like the people who have hurt me; that one day, I will mistake my hairy arms as his, my voice as one that swallowed my own. From the beginning, these men tricked me into thinking that my body was theirs. This book has been a process of writing a future in which I can address and reclaim what is mine. *To my voice, if we had a better relationship, maybe I never would have left you that night.*

I carved out space for this anthology, specifically for fellow trans and non-binary survivors, because we have all been told at some point, "Why don't you write about something else?" We are ruptures to someone else's matrix. Our bodies are not embarrassments; our stories cannot fit into a shape assigned at birth. We are not a loss of potential. On my first day of class, a teacher named Brad Calcaterra told me, "You are the future." To all of the writers of this book, trust that I also think that of you. You are the future; keep writing yourself in when there are people in this world who really believe they can erase you.

I write this to my future. *To my voice, I know you're never gone.* My pieces and yours, they're here in the pages living, living as a body of work, perhaps for the first time in your life, as something you can hold.

GUIDE FOR PROFESSIONALS AND MENTORS

by Ieshai Bailey, LMHC, CST

Hey you. Yes, the one who is reading this. This part. Are you a helping professional? Mentor? Coach? However, you identify professionally, I ask you to take some time and embrace what you have just read and then after you have done that...breathe...

I want to start off by sharing this wasn't an easy task for me to do. Well, not like I thought it would be. I was asked to write a guide by Lexie and I had this idea I knew exactly what I would write. I remember our initial conversation as Lexie prompted me to write to my parts...and if you're wondering...well I did. As a person who works extensively with the Gender Variant community, I found myself feeling a flood of emotions I haven't felt in a very long time. And then I began to have a greater appreciation (even more than I already had) for the work I do. After reading this anthology, you may too.

As you take the time to read and, hopefully, re-read the stories, I encourage you to utilize what I have included in this guide. Regardless of how you identify within the community: Advocate, Ally, Clinical professional, or all of the above, take your time with exploring your own feelings. However, before you explore, I am going to ask that you complete these steps:

First, I implore you to put aside everything you may think you know about the Gender Variant Community. Yes, just drop it right out of your mind! And don't worry, you can pick it up later. As you read each letter, word, sentence, paragraph, and dialogue, you have a unique opportunity to do the most single important thing I am going to ask you to do right now and that is: LISTEN.

Oftentimes, when we are tasked with meeting our clients, we meet them in vulnerable spaces. Spaces of pain, spaces filled with passion, spaces of perseverance. We are tasked to be the "experts" providing them with tools and techniques they can use to heal, overcome, and change. But oftentimes, we may not provide the level of "safety" that is needed in order to do so. Well at least, not initially. For many Trans- and Non Binary-identified individuals, reaching out for help is difficult. When carrying a traumatic past, individuals may be reluctant to seek help due to fear of being "outed," and discriminated against, as well as the fear of professionals seeking to "cure them." It is not uncommon for clients to report discrimination and abuse while living in shelters and transitional housing. They have reported mistreatment when seeking help at mental health facilities, hospitals, and even organizations that promote gender and sexual inclusivity. Due to this, Trans and Non Binary clients may come to you with a distrust of you and a distrust of the process. They may fear for their safety, feel isolated, and have an overall sense of skepticism despite your greatest efforts.

This is why it is extremely important for you to listen to what your client will report, as well as what they do not report. It is crucial for you to understand that every client's story will be unique. Perhaps the theme will the same (i.e. discrimination, oppression, abuse, trauma), but the experience is distinct to them. Therefore, when using this anthology as a guide, start by refocusing on having your own clients speak to themselves in ways which give them a voice. Encourage them to speak to the parts of themselves which may have been lost or remained mute because of what they endured. Consider using or presenting this book to your clients as a handheld support group to combat feelings of isolation. Then consider using your own techniques to help the client feel safe, feel heard, and feel validated.

Yes, I know, I know. Sometimes the constraints of a professional or personal time may not allow it. We get so hung up on 50-minute sessions, co-pays, current procedural terminology codes, techniques, medical education, and psycho-education, we may miss the chance of listening to our clients. Staying silent and actually listening. This is the reason the words "SILENT" and "LISTEN" share the same letters. Do you see it? It's not a coincidence.

In order to listen, and I mean listen with care, we must remain silent. We must allow each person to speak their truth, speak to parts of themselves in order to reclaim what they felt may have been taken from them. When you allow each person to take the time to develop a relationship with themselves—their whole self—listen to what they say.

After you have stayed silent, listened, and provided a feeling of safety for your client, I am going to ask you to use these pages as a tool to break barriers of dialogue. Many of the writers are able to create a different narrative by writing "to" their body parts instead of "about" their body parts. The narrative becomes a reflection of the non-verbal communication our bodies often speak. An identity of a single part, which may have once been objectified, misused, abused, dehumanized, medicalized, hidden, and hurt. You may be able to ask your own clients to write to their body part(s) in ways which provide support, nurturance, and guidance. Help guide them to talk about themselves or parts of themselves offering support, protection, and forgiveness.

Next, I would like for you to assess the level of privilege you have over your clients. Remember when I told you clients often come to us in vulnerable spaces? They seek out our expertise and we, as the professional, often do a great job at sharing all we know. We can diagnose, educate, prescribe, and refer. Whether you are a sex therapist, medical doctor, mentor, clinical social worker, or psychiatrist, you hold that privilege, you are recognized as the expert. We have years of life experiences and schooling: masters degrees, medical degrees, and PhDs. So, in some regards we are the experts, right? But are we?

By using this as a guide, it can help each of us to realize our clients have a PhD in their own lives! They have depicted expertise in pain, expertise in wanting to live an authentic life, expertise at hiding, covering, expertise at wanting to be who they are: human. They have explored and displayed perseverance and empowerment. How are your clients empowered?

I even urge you, as you reflect back on the stories, to ask yourself how many times have you written to your mind? To your stomach? To your eyes? Legs? Genitals? If you did, what would you say? Now imagine each of these parts had an opportunity to respond. What would they say back to you?

Moving on, perhaps you have encountered difficulty in engaging in dialogue with someone who has experienced trauma. Trauma, in the simplest form, is defined as a deeply disturbing or distressing event which can be physical, mental, emotional, sexual, and even spiritual. The biggest hurdle you may encounter with trauma and trauma survivors is shame and guilt, as well as the lack of power and control. A survivor is defined within this context as a person who has coped with or overcome difficulties or deeply disturbing and distressing events in their life.

When talking to survivors, one may receive negative messages about their bodies. Messages regarding the lack of boundaries, their bodies being "wrong" and "different," or their bodies are their identity rather than who they are. Oftentimes with these messages, survivors can feel betrayed by others, or as if their bodies have betrayed them. This, as you can imagine, may be a difficult thing to live with. This anthology can help your client express this through writing, with you being there to understand what they are communicating to you. Can you hear them?

I can imagine you being a reader who reads in silence; or a reader who likes to read out loud. Whatever your preference, remember what I asked in the beginning? What are your feelings now? Have you listened? Have you remained silent? Take some time to review the following terms I have included in this guide and then ask yourself what this anthology can do for you. Don't worry, I am here, I am listening, I am silent.

TERMS TO KNOW
Transgender/Trans: an encompassing term or "umbrella term" of many gender identities who do not identify, or

solely identify, with the sex they were assigned with at birth.

Cisgender: a term for someone whose gender identity exclusively aligns with the sex which they were assigned to at birth.

Gender Identity: an individual's internal sense of what it means being a male or female or boy or girl, neither, or both. Please note: gender identity is not the same as sexual orientation/sexual identity.

Non-Binary: an umbrella term for all genders other than male/female or woman/man, boy/girl. Please note: not all Non-Binary individuals identify as Trans and not all Trans people identify as Non-Binary.

Survivor: a person who has coped with or overcome difficulties which would have resulted in the death of another in the same event or a person who has prevailed over deeply disturbing and distressing events in their life.

Trauma: a deeply disturbing or distressing event. This can be mental, physical, emotional, sexual, spiritual, or a combination of any of these.

USEFUL WEBSITES

Below are a list of websites with more terms and information relating to gender identity:

www.glaad.org

www.genderdiversity.org

www.transequality.org

LETTER WRITERS ON THEIR LETTER WRITING EXPERIENCE

"It was something i didn't know i needed. Accidental medicine."

—*Chello*

"I have felt a deep sense of liberation since writing this piece. A dear friend of mine once told me that, for him, unnamed sexual assault was the "last thing sitting on top of your voice." It's true for my voice too. Once I named what I need to name, from my childhood and early adolescence, it was as if there was nothing I couldn't say.

The essay also became part of my perpetual "coming out" process for me, as a nonbinary person who is not pursuing medical treatment. My "transition" will necessarily be in writing and art and performance, and so every naming and expression of my inner state becomes a part of that.

Thank you, Lexie Bean, for this liberating opportunity."

—*Chloé Rossetti*

"I feel a lot of pressure for things to always be getting better, especially internal/personal things. Writing these letters was an opportunity to be hopeful but still honest—to reckon with myself where I am, not where I think I should be."

—*Anonymous*

"i wrote my piece years ago. it feels like a different human, a different me.

it's a reminder that i'm always having to make peace with not being all of my selves at once..."

—*Anonymous*

"Trauma frequently feels very personal, and sometimes that's a good thing, but writing for this anthology helped my trauma feel less personal. I am one of many trans and nonbinary writers who are working on healing and we, as a squadron, can help ourselves, each other, and readers of the anthology heal. That feels powerful in a way I could not achieve alone."

—*Anonymous*

AUTHORS

This book holds one to three parts and pieces from the following people:

A.D. Sean Lewis
Alex DiFrancesco
Alex Olkovsky
Alex Valdes
Alison Kronstadt
Byron James Kimball
Chello Solaperto
Chloé Rossetti
Chris Segal
Corbin Went
Diane Sparkes
Eddy Funkhouser
Esther Roth-Colson
Evelyn Deshane
Fforest
Harish Iyer
HJ Farr
Jak
Jamie Beckenstein
Jamie Bushell

Jennie Pajerowski
Julian Mithra
Kai Cheng Thom
Karalyn E. Pearl Grimes
Kate Morgan
Kye Campbell-Fox
Laura S
Lexie Bean
L. Munir
Meghan Blythe Adams
Nyala Moon
Orion Benedict
Rachael Ysera
Sarah Bernstein
Sasha Gough
Sawyer DeVuyst
Sebastian Zulch
Sol Ramos
Summer Minerva
hu-yang 胡杨

One person wishes to remain anonymous.

ADDITIONAL PIECES AND GUIDES BY:

Dean Spade

Dean Spade is the author of *Normal Life: Administrative Violence, Critical Trans Politics and the Limits of Law* (Duke 2015).

His writing and videos can be found at deanspade.net.

Nyala Moon

Nyala Moon is an aspiring actor, writer and producer. She recently finished her Bachelors of Arts at Baruch College this past May. Nyala has always been a performer at heart but didn't think it was space for a black transgender woman like herself. Nyala is a New York native with southern roots. Nyala has had a love affair with cinema ever since she first saw *Casablanca* and *The Good, the Bad and the Ugly* with her grandparents. Now that Nyala has finished her education, she is ready to openly pursue her love affair with cinema by telling queer stories because she believes little black transgirls shouldn't grow up and not see a reflection of themselves in the media.

Alex Valdes

Alex Valdes is an experimental musician, performance artist, and Brooklyn, NY native. Using drag spectacle and power electronics as their alter ego, Reagan Holiday, they continue to explore the dissonance, pain, and beauty of the trans masculine experience.

See more of them @reaganholiday on Instagram.

Lexie Bean

Writer, performer, Myers Briggs INFJ, and breakfast advocate based in Queens, NY. This is their third anthology full of letters people have written to their body parts. From writing for *Teen Vogue*, to documentary-making, to leading two international workshop and performance tours—much of their work revolves around themes of bodies, homes, cyclical violence, and queer foreshadowing. Next moves include writing a children's book and eating more pizza.

Say hi at www.lexiebean.com or @oklexiebean on Instagram.

Sawyer DeVuyst

Visual artist, model and actor, Leo, and a middle child. His work aspires to empower and humanize otherized communities through visibility and storytelling. He previously partnered with Thinx's "People with Periods" Campaign and HBO's *Vice* to discuss trans masculine representation in the media. He is currently living and working out of Los Angeles and Brooklyn, and continuing his daily fine art self-portrait collection, "Mine."

To see the growing collection, visit @sawyermine on Instagram or www.sawyerdevuyst.com.

Ieshai Bailey

LMHC, CST, is a PhD candidate in Clinical Sexology, Board Certified Sex Therapist, Board Certified Transgender Care Therapist, Licensed Medical Mental Health Counselor, Sexuality

Educator, Advocate, and Speaker working in private practice. Specializing with Gender Variant and Sexual Variant Community, Ieshai focuses on providing "affirming psychotherapy" for a variety of concerns, including relationship dynamics, LGBTQI concerns, fetishes, kink, military issues, infidelity/cheating.

For more information, please feel free to visit www.bhowyou.com.

LOVE TO...

The folks who donated to my original gofundme page to get this variation of the project off the ground in summer of 2016. It was my first coming out as trans in a relatively public way. Your donations and encouragement in your own special ways continue to give me longevity and hope: Savannah Rose Crespo, Jessica Lam, Leah Johnson, Tanya Lyon, Harley Bosco, David Tisel, Zofii Kaczmarek, Christine Walden, Amy Campbell, Dani Miriti Pacheco, Stephen Dexter, Molly Bennett, Stevie Kelly, Felix Hiciano, Jake Kosinski, Ilona Brand, Dana Levinson, Hope Goodrich, Maya Iverson, Laura Jessee Livingston, Conrad Schlör, Shoshana Gordon, Kira Goldner, Eddy Funkhouser, Lena Amick, Max Cosmo, Hilary Neff, Clara Lincoln, Kristiana Graves, Alice Lubeck, Cory Todd, Dan Laufer, Henry Towbin, Stephanie Koehler, Lizzie Roberts, Annie Rasiel, and Connor Stratton.

All the writers of my first two anthologies, *Attention: People with Body Parts* and *Portable Homes*, for sitting with yourselves, sitting together, and witnessing growth. In the most literal way, this book wouldn't have happened without you trusting me and this process. Big huge feelings for the sweet humans who toured with *Portable Homes* and co-facilitated or co-created events with me over the years, including Sarah Cheshire, Caroline Mills, Meredith Siefert, David Zager, Laura Grothaus, Rosalie Eck, Amanda Jacir, Sam Fisher, Akane Little, Karalyn Grimes, Laura Shriver, Amethyst Carey, Zia Kandler, Heather Loschen, Sasha Gough, Yoshimi, and Lexi Gee. Lisa Neumann for trusting my wacky post-grad vision and telling me that I'm full of rain. Heather Sedlacek for trusting my other wacky post-grad vision and telling me that I'm an ocean. Former professors Meredith Raimondo, Baron Pineda, DeSales Harrison, Harrod Suarez, Kazim Ali, and Ann Cooper Albright for being the first adults to affirm my project that seemed so far from schoolwork.

Tails Williams for telling me, "You need to publish this book," in 2012. Karmilla Pillay-Siokos for telling me, "You need to publish this book," again in 2016.

Shelby Ziesing for making me a space-themed crown when I was feeling diasporic and anxious about going outside. Daniel Lobb, Rowan Bassman, Paavo Poutiainen, and Lila Leatherman for being from the same planet as me. Tanya Stickles for reassuring me that it is okay to write about what I want to write about. Alison Kronstadt for reassuring me with your beautiful thesaurus heart full of pep talks. MJ Robinson, at the time an almost-stranger, for being the first person I confided in for wanting top surgery. Charlie Peck, at the time a real-stranger, for teaching me that change is not loss. Tomasz Deeg, Sawyer DeVuyst, Alex Valdes, James Vitz-Wong, Adriel Irizarry, Chad Luke Schiro, Jax Jackson, Linus Ignatius, Chloé Rossetti, Sky Scholfield, Amos Wolff, Vikas Satyal, Wolf Pulsiano, and Luke Burns, who give me courage to navigate what it means to be a boy or a boy-ish. Summer Pilaf and JP Moraga for your fluidity and groundedness. Kelsey Scult for sending me

a Mr. Potato Head, Jonas Becker for sending me a black
and blue book, and Ashley Miller for sending me butterfly
wings in the mail when I was sad. Joslyn DeFreece for
reminding me of all the ways I can help myself. Wren
Leader, Ali Leibowitz, Alison Cameron, and Mieko Gavia
for being overall very, very good. Nyala Moon, who gets
ten gold stars. Stuti Das, Ayush Mukherjee, Kevin Necciai,
Wesley Alexander, and Christof Milando for being true
cheerleaders and offering questions that gave me energy
along the way. Tina Hanaé, the accountability all-star.
C Bain for your poetry wizardry. Laurie Halse Anderson,
Andrea Gibson, sj Miller, and Dean Spade for reaching
back, and offering words worthy of cross-stitching. Ieshai
Bailey and Tamara Williams for your super-human
strength and will to try new things.

Anthony Ritosa, Ian Fields Stewart, and all the folks
curating loving and vital spaces for facilitated dialogue
with @Salon. Yasemin Ozumerzifon and Amy Miller at
Gibney Dance for spearheading the ICAT Program, as well
as your openness to meet and collaborate when my ideas
seemed like just little seeds.

Sue Shapiro, Elizabeth Kuhr, Annie Field, Paul Moon,
and Aspen Matis for always encouraging me to share my
writing, especially when I am afraid of my own words.
Vera Papisova at *Teen Vogue*, Lisa Factora-Borchers at *Bitch*
Magazine, Nikki Gloudeman at *The Establishment*, Erika
Smith at *BUST* magazine, Alexa Strabuk at *Ms.* magazine,
Beenish Ahmed, Zoe Holman, and all the other editors
and journalists who made space for this project within
their publications, bringing in at least half of the writers
of this anthology. Erin Elizabeth Smith at Firefly Farms for
including me in your writers residency program, and my
mom for encouraging me to go. Krista Cox, Beth Couture,
Stacey Balkrun, and Jennie Frost for facilitating the

workshops that gave me the push I needed to finally write
my own letters to my body parts after nearly six months
of collecting pieces from other people. Troy Spindler and
Victoria Cox for drinking milkshakes with me at a park
bench in Tennessee at the tail-end of the workshop and
residency, and Tom Rathe for driving me there.

Elizabeth Koke with Housing Works and William Johnson
with Lambda Literary for your kindness and sparkle. You
ultimately led me to meet Andrew James, Sean Townsend,
and the Jessica Kingsley Publishers Team.

Emily Clarke, David Roswell, Kevin Dee, Katherine Mowrer,
and Aaron Krupp for being real super stars in helping me
navigate my relationship with therapy, my transition, and
my ability to ask for help. Thank you for supporting me
to find my own ways to pay it forward. Susan Rice and
Charlie Gross for creating healthy, un-closeted, working
environments. Chloe Glickman, Zettie Shapey, and Rena
Branson, I shed lil tears whenever I think about you. Z,
Alli, J, and the rest of the Redwoods Circle for teaching
me (and their world) about teamwork, and singing "Love
More" on my favorite wooden floor. Elizabeth Roberge for
sponsoring my high school's Gay-Straight Alliance, even
under the pressure of an unsupportive administration and
student-body; you knew my friends and I were just looking
for a safe place to go after school. Robert Russell for always
reminding me to stay in the boat. Brad Calcaterra and
the Act Out community for creating a pact and teaching
me how to walk into a room with the decision that I
belong there.

My lil community of Gab Spear, Leanna Burton, John
Tournas, and Miga Ochir, who make sure I eat, go to sleep,
and keep good things consistent in my life. My teammate
Jamie Firman for getting balloons on that worst day and

helping me believe in a better future in which every part of us survives. Lastly, I want to acknowledge those who have tried to push me so far from my truths that I had to work this hard to ground myself in my own.

RESOURCES

AUSTRALIA
A Gender Agenda: www.genderrights.org.au
Public awareness group on sex and gender diversity issues focusing on training, support services, and law reform.

Gender Help for Parents: www.genderhelpforparents.com.au
Extensive lists of services and support groups for families with trans children.

Minus18: www.minus18.org.au
Australia's largest youth-led organization for LGBTQ youth.

Transgender Victoria: www.transgendervictoria.com
Dedicated to seeking justice, equity and quality health and community services for trans people, their families, and friends.

QLife: www.qlife.org.au
Nationwide phone and online chat counseling for LGBTQ people, 3 pm to midnight every day. 1800 184 527.

CANADA

The 519: www.the519.org
LGBTQ community center offering services, spaces for community organizing, trainings, and legal consultations.

Buddies in Bad Times Theatre: www. buddiesinbadtimes.com/community/youth
Toronto-based free training and mentoring program for queer and trans youth (30 and under) with interest in creating theater and performance work.

Gender Spectrum: https://genderspectrum.org
Organizers of conferences and public trainings on creating gender-sensitive and inclusive environments.

Project 10/Projet 10: www.p10.qc.ca
Advocacy and information center for LGBTQ and two-spirit youth (25 and younger) in Montreal. They also offer an anonymous listening line at 514-989-4585 every Tuesday through Thursday, 12 pm to 6 pm.

Trans Lifeline: www.translifeline.org
24/7 hotline by trans people and for trans people who are in crisis and/or are struggling with identity. Canada line: 877 330 6366. Also available 24/7 in the USA: 877-565-8860.

Transgender Health Information Program: www.transhealth.phsa.ca
Hub for finding gender-affirming care and health services across British Columbia.

**Two Spirit Resource Directory: www.nativeyouth
sexualhealth.com/twospiritdirectory.html**
Community organizing, mentorship, education
programming, and media resource list for two-spirit
Native Americans.

Qmunity: www.qmunity.ca
British Columbia resource guide for LGBTQ and two-spirit
folks for support, taking action, and social opportunities.

IRELAND
BeLonG To: www.belongto.org
Support services for LGBTQ youth nationwide, including
counseling, and information for asylum-seekers.

LGBT Helpline: www.lgbt.ie
Confidential hotline for LGBT people and their families
looking for additional listening and support. 1890 929 539.

Outhouse: www.outhouse.ie
Community center for LGBT Dubliners seeking events,
connection, and opportunities to organize.

Transgender Equality Network Ireland: www.teni.ie
National network promoting rights and resources for trans
folks and their families.

UK
All about Trans: www.allabouttrans.org.uk
Project challenging and changing mainstream media
understanding and portrayals of trans people. Site also
has an extensive list of support organizations throughout
London and the UK.

Edinburgh Trans Women: www. edinburghtranswomen.org.uk
Monthly support group and hosts for social events for trans women in Edinburgh.

Mermaids: www.mermaidsuk.org.uk
Awareness group supporting gender nonconforming and trans children. Aiming to improve training and resources for families, schools, and social services.

Scottish Trans Alliance: www.scottishtrans.org
Assisting trans people in connecting with service providers, employers, and equality organizations.

UK Trans Info: www.uktrans.info
Website pooling together resources for public sector organizations, activists, and individuals seeking community support.

World Help Lines: www.worldhelplines.org/uk.html
Extensive list of hotlines for LGBT people, survivors of domestic abuse and sexual assault, as well as kids, runaways, and those in suicide crisis.

USA
Anti-Violence Project: www.avp.org
Organizing, education, and outreach for community members who experience anti-LGBTQ* violence. Includes client services, economic advocacy, legal support, and a national coalition of anti-violence programming.

Audre Lorde Project: www.alp.org
Working with LGB, Two Spirit, and trans and non-binary people of color towards education and capacity building, community wellness, and social and economic justice.

Black and Pink: www.blackandpink.org
Support program for LGBTQ prisoners and their allies
to respond with advocacy, education, direct service, and
organizing.

Forge: www.forge-forward.org
National anti-violence organization offering direct
services to trans and non-binary survivors of sexual
assault. They develop extensive trauma-informed tool-kits
and training events for service providers who work with
trans and non-binary survivors.

Generation FIVE: www.generationfive.org
Anti-violence organization combating child sexual
abuse and larger systems of oppression through creative
educational programming.

LGBT National Help Center Hotline: www.glnh.org
Free and confidential helpline for all ages. National
hotline: 888-843-4564. Youth talkline: 800-246-7743.

The Icarus Project: www.theicarusproject.net
A support network and education project by and for
people who experience the world in ways often diagnosed
as mental illness. They offer workshops, webinars, peer
support spaces, and publications on self-care and
community care.

INCITE!: www.incite-national.org
National activist organization of women, gender non-
conforming, and trans people of color. They advance a
movement to end violence against their communities
through direct action, critical dialogue, and grassroots
organizing.

Lighthouse: www.lighthouse.lgbt
LGBTQ* affirming healthcare provider search engine, including therapists, psychologists, primary, care, surgeons, etc.

National Center for Transgender Equality: www.transequality.org
Group focused on policy change. They offer fact-sheets and legal tips for trans people navigating federal institutions.

Planet Deafqueer: www.planet.deafqueer.com
Resources by and for deaf queer communities, including pages specific to youth and trans people.

Rad Remedy: www.radremedy.org
Site and zine-maker dedicated to connecting trans, non-binary, intersex, and queer folks to accurate, safe, respectful, and compressive healthcare.

Sex Workers Outreach Project— USA: www.new.swopusa.org
Social justice network dedicated to fundamental human rights of people involved in sex work and their communities, tackling violence and stigma through advocacy and education.

Survived and Punished: www.survivedandpunished.org
National organizing project formed by coalition of feminist anti-prison advocates and defense campaigns to support criminalized survivors and abolish gender violence, policing, prisons, and deportations.

Queers for Economic Justice:
www.queersforeconmicjustice.org
NYC shelter organizing project and advocacy group for
homeless and low-income LGBT people.

Sylvia Rivera Law Project: www.srlp.org
Free legal services for low-income trans and non-binary
folks and people of color. Includes a Prisoner Advisory
Committee made up of trans people and allies who are
currently incarcerated.

Trevor Project: www.thetrevorproject.com
Crisis hotline and suicide prevention for LGBTQ* youth
(13–24 years old): 866-488-7386.

FURTHER READING

RELATED ANTHOLOGIES
Portable Homes, by Lexie Bean.

Attention: People with Body Parts, by Lexie Bean.

Color of Violence: The INCITE! Anthology, by INCITE!, Duke University Press.

Queering Sexual Violence: Radical Voices from within the Anti-Violence Movement, by Jennifer Patterson, Riverdale Avenue Books.

TRANS, NON-BINARY, AND QUEER PEOPLE ON TRAUMA AND SURVIVAL
My, My, My, My by Tara Hardy, Write Bloody Publishing.

My Dad Thinks I'm a Boy?! by Sophie Labelle.

Dirty River: A Queer Femme of Color Dreaming Her Way Home, by Leah Lakshmi, Arsenal Pulp Press.

Femme in Public, by Alok Vaid-Menon.

RESOURCES FOR PROFESSIONALS, MENTORS, AND SELF

Meet Polkadot, by Talcott Broadhead.

The Revolution Starts at Home: Confronting Intimate Violence within Activist Communities, by Ching-In Chen, Jai Dulani, and Leah Lakshmi Piepzna-Samarasinha, AK Press.

Trans Bodies, Trans Selves: A Resource for Trans Community, by Laura Erickson-Schroth, Oxford University Press.

Teaching, Affirming, and Recognizing Trans and Gender Creative Youth, by sj Miller, Palgrave Macmillan.